PEAK
PERSISTENCE

Why Some Reach Life's Summits

While Others Fail

DAVID SNOW

Printed in the United States of America
First Printing 2020
First Edition 2020

ISBN: 979-8632709668

10 9 8 7 6 5 4 3 2 1

Cover photo by David Snow: Tom Wilkinson and Gyaljen Sherpa
climbing the Yellow Band on the Lhotse Face, Mt Everest
Edited by Christopher Murray

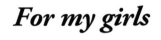

For my girls

TABLE OF CONTENTS

INTRODUCTION

Nothing in the world can take the place of persistence. Talent will not; nothing is more common than unsuccessful men with talent. Genius will not; unrewarded genius is almost a proverb... Persistence and determination alone are omnipotent.

- Calvin Coolidge 30th President of the United States

We can't turn back. I won't turn back. Winds that have pounded us at 60 miles per hour for the past seven hours now increase again, unleashing 100 mph bursts with no protection offered on the exposed South Summit of Mt. Everest. It's 3:30 a.m. The valves of our oxygen masks flutter open and closed; isolated in the desolate landscape, we wait. Sarki has been on the radio back to Base Camp requesting weather updates. Our Base Camp manager, Lhakpa, responds finally from the other end, his voice barely distinguishable above the howling wind, saying the winds and forecasted weather are too strong; he tells us to abandon our summit attempt.

Just 300 vertical feet separate us from our goal of reaching the rooftop of the world. An achievement that has occupied some portion of my thoughts, each day, for the better part of four years. As the expedition leader, I've organized climbs every year for my friends and me to the highest points on every continent, and each year we were successful in reaching the summit. This would be our culminating climb, the last and final of the Seven Summits—the highest peak on each of the seven continents.

Our base camp manager and friend, Lhakpa Gelu Sherpa, is a legend on Everest. He has summited Everest 15 times while holding the Guinness Book of World Records for the fastest summit speed ascent on Everest in an unfathomable 10 hours 56 minutes from base camp to summit—a process normally taking 4 to 5 days for a standard expedition. I met Lhakpa years earlier on Mt. Rainier. He stood out because he was wearing a black garbage bag as a poncho to shelter his down coat from the sleet, all the while running from tent to tent assisting his clients before their summit ahead. We became fast friends and now found ourselves halfway across the world on Everest. Our team was in our seventh hour of climbing to the summit, relying on Lhakpa's information from 11,000 feet below. Months before our expedition, Lhakpa said, "May 17th is a lucky day," then added, grinning and speaking in his thick Nepali accent, "We don't even need forecast." And now, here we are on the 17th of May with a vertical length of a football field to go.

For the better part of two weeks, the entire South side of Mt. Everest was anxiously awaiting the Sherpa Rope Team, a group of expert climbing Sherpas responsible for securing fixed climbing rope all the way from the South Col (also known as Camp 4) to the summit, to complete their work. No climber could move ahead of the rope team, and all were at their mercy to finish the ropes so that this year's climbers could safely clip into the mountain's lifeline and ascend to the summit. Poor weather, poor delegation, and fighting amongst the major guiding outfits on who should bear most of the cost and effort to fix the lines created delays in the summit ropes for several weeks. World-famous Everest blogger

Alan Arnett described the 2017 Everest climbing season as "one of the more difficult seasons I have covered to sum up in one word, so let me use several: wind, tragedy, misinformation, spin, and summits."

Standing on the most famous piece of real estate in the world had individual significance for all of us. My best friend, Tom, whom I've known since our junior year in high school, had just finalized his divorce from a brief marriage and was looking at putting some things behind him while also looking to complete his sixth of the Seven Summits. Following in his family's rich heritage as Delta Airline pilots, Tom is a captain with the company. With a quick wit, ready smile, and offbeat sense of humor, he is the perfect traveling companion, climbing partner, and tentmate. Tom seems to eat the miles with ease, striding effortlessly forward. Bundled up in a tent, hour-after-hour, day-after-day, would drive anyone insane, but thankfully I had Tom to keep it light.

Larry, having just finished the longest Iditarod in history, was set to become the first person to ever summit Everest and complete the Iditarod in the same year. Living in Alaska, Larry is a non-stop stockpile of optimism, always looking for the next adventure. Tough as nails in extreme environments, he still manages to be a family man who spends his time adventuring with the kids. Larry is a Radiation Oncologist and, along with Brandon, founder of Radiating Hope, a nonprofit organization that raises money to supply radiation equipment for therapy and cancer screening and treatment in third world countries.

For Brandon, the strongest climber in our group, mountain climbing had become an all-consuming passion, leading to pitched battles at home. His focus, strength, and determination are unmatched in the mountains. Prone at times to be reserved and uncommunicative, yet kind at heart, his sheer force of will and undaunting belief have led us to many summits. Our friendship continues to grow to this day.

For me, this would be my final summit of the Seven Summits, achieving a mountain climbing milestone that few achieve.

Preparing for the summit of big mountains is a unique endeavor. On Everest, everyone is trying to decipher and interpret the weather forecast. For only a brief few weeks every year, the jet stream that rips across Everest's summit shifts, allowing, hopefully, a weather window to reach the top. Timing is everything since it can take up to five days of climbing to summit. Most expeditions target a particular day 4-5 days out and begin the climb up the mountain staging at the various camps. With the extreme conditions and oppressive altitude, teams can't afford to spend time waiting out storms high on the mountain—the resources are just not there, and the bodies of team members would be in a constant state of deterioration. Everything is designed to have the team staged at Camp 4, briefly resting, then beginning the summit push late at night when the winds abate, affording a shot at the top. It is a true balancing act. Leave too early and you'll spend most of the ascent freezing and risking frostbite in the darkness. Leave too late, and you may not make it off the summit in time to return to Camp 4 before darkness descends again. With Himalayan weather changing daily, aligning the right weather for the summit is a mission in itself.

On May 13th, we had departed Everest base camp at 17,500 feet, deciding to bypass Camp 1 and head straight for Camp 2. We were late out of base camp, which put us above the Khumbu Icefall around 10 a.m. The Khumbu Icefall is a treacherous area of falling ice, gaping crevasses, and overhanging seracs that seem destined to collapse at any moment (and sometimes do). In 2014, 16 Sherpas lost their lives in this section due to an avalanche. In 2015, an earthquake caused another avalanche killing 22 people in the icefall and surrounding areas near base camp. It's an area in which even the best climbers can disappear. Nobody enters the icefall without trepidation or the desire to pass through as quickly as possible.

We soon entered the Western Cwm (pronounced "koom"), a broad, flat glacier, just as the morning rays began preheating the world's largest convection oven. With no wind and temperatures at a stale 100 degrees Fahrenheit, my down summit suit turned into a personal steam room, so I was forced to fold it over and tie the top half around my waist. Our water had run out hours ago, and we became so focused on thirst that it brought our group to a standstill. A dangerously dehydrated Tom could no longer continue, so we radioed to Camp 2 for someone to bring water down immediately. That immediacy took about an hour, and it was far overdue. This was NOT the way we planned to arrive at the end of Day 1 for our five-day summit push!

We rested for two nights at Camp 2, drinking and eating with little appetite. The cruel phenomenon that falls upon most climbers at high altitude is a diminished appetite. The higher you get, the more it increases. And though your body is starved for calories, it's at this point when you need it most. I was facing another dish comprised of rice and lentils known as dal bhat. An uncontrolled gag reflex accompanied every bite, since it was the fifth straight week of eating similar food, spiced exactly the same way. Leaving camp in the morning, we made our approach to the Lhotse Face, a 2500-foot wall of sheer ice, peppered with bands of rock. The rope Sherpas had fixed lines here, and we ponderously made our way to Camp 3, which is perched on a small ledge positioned in the middle of the Lhotse face.

On May 16th, at 6 a.m., we set out for our final camp, the South Col. We finally received confirmation that the summit rope Sherpas had just completed fixing the lines to the summit. We had gambled that they would, and that we'd be numbered among the first groups attempting the summit this season.

Arriving in Camp 4 around noon, we settled in and made our last supper (not literally, I hoped). I began to write in my pocket-sized yellow waterproof notebook those things I wanted to remember at the summit—thanking sponsors and my loved ones whom I wanted to recognize for getting me there—just in case the air was too thin and recalling the obvious wasn't so obvious. That was my mindset. I didn't allow the possibility of not summiting to enter or consume my thoughts. Like so many times before, I envisioned myself on the summit and was preparing to express my gratitude coherently.

After a while, I called out to Brandon and Larry and asked them to join Tom and me in our tent. I let them know how proud I was of the preparation and determination of our climbing team. Five months previously, on New Year's Day, I broke the news to my daughters that I was climbing Everest. The two younger daughters shouted with joy, tried on my overflowing orange summit suit, and began to ask all the questions that you'd expect from a 9- and 11-year-old: when are you going, who's going, how cold does it get, your Everest outfit looks like a pumpkin! However, my 13-year-old didn't say a word. She quietly left, and my wife motioned to go talk with her. Following her to her room, she lay on her bed, and she did her best to hold it in but started sobbing, saying, "I just don't want to lose you." My daughters have grown up their entire lives with their father climbing big mountains, but Everest and all its perceptions and misconceptions were circling in the mind of my oldest. After pulling my heart out from the bottom of my throat long enough to speak, I made her a promise. I said that, without a doubt, we would be the most prepared team on Everest.

And we were.

Sitting in the tent at Camp 4, I reiterated that story to my friends and thanked them for keeping that promise. With winds relentlessly pounding the tent, guy-lines snapping like rubber bands, we tried to combat the ever-present pressure squeezing our brains caused by the limited available air, reminding us that we were in the Death Zone—an area where no living thing can survive. What could I say to my buddies who'd been with me on every continent and in every climbing and weather situation, poised at the precipice of our biggest test? I removed my oxygen mask and read a poem I had written down long ago on the last page of my yellow pocket notebook. I felt it appropriate in this moment:

Invictus

Out of the night that covers me,

Black as the pit from pole to pole

I thank whatever Gods may be

For my unconquerable soul.

In the fell clutch of circumstance

I have not winced nor cried aloud

Under the bludgeoning of chance

My head is bloody, but unbowed

Beyond this place of wrath and tears

Looms but the horror of the shade

And yet the menace of the years

Finds and shall find me unafraid

It matters not how strait the gate

How charged with punishments the scroll

I am the master of my fate

I am the captain of my soul

-William Henley 1875

Brandon snapped a picture of this poem and retreated to his tent, and then the waiting began in earnest. For the next few hours, we did our best impression of sleeping. But it was in vain. Of all the times we needed a rested body, it was now. But the environment, the excitement, my resting heart rate of 120 beats per minute, and the discomfort of the oxygen mask forbade it.

In the midst of our summit push through the Khumbu Icefall, we encountered a Frenchman with his sights set on summiting without oxygen; he was on an acclimating climb. When hearing of our chosen summit date, he said, "17 May is no good, winds too strong." Lhakpa Sherpa's forecast indicated the jet stream with its 100 mph winds would shift and while, although windy, he advised us to make a push for the summit arriving before 7:00 a.m. This would allow us to beat the next storm front approaching before it slammed the door shut on the summit for many days to follow. So far, the winds were furious but climbable.

There was another problem in our camp. Our guides had forgotten an important lifeline—fuel for our stove. Without it, the snow at Camp 4 couldn't be melted for the precious water we needed now, on the summit push, and on the return. The water we were to take for the summit was now left to what we had in our reserves and what our guides could beg and borrow from other Sherpas nearby. I had 1.5 liters of water to last me the next 24 hours of nonstop climbing.

With sleep not to be found, I lay envisioning the path I'd seen dozens of times in my mind, the final steps onto the summit proper … Suddenly, our lead guide, Sarki Sherpa, snapped me back to reality, shouting above the wind that it was time to make ready.

We began the hour-long process of getting dressed: putting warm feet covered with thick socks into frozen plastic boots; slipping on a glove liner, followed by a down inner glove and then an outer expedition glove; adjusting oxygen masks; zipping up the back sides and front of the summit suits; carefully situating energy gels and water bottles for easier access while climbing; loading final camera batteries; checking harness buckles; strapping on crampons; securing caps; placing headlamps on helmets; putting on clear goggles; and putting in our backpack compartments any mementos to place or photograph at the summit.

By 9:00 p.m., Larry and Brandon were ready and waiting while Tom and I were another 15 minutes before we were prepared to head out. Larry said they were freezing up and need to get started, so he offered a quick prayer for us all and he and Brandon headed for the rooftop of the world, following behind Sarki, who set the pace and had to wade through calf- to thigh-high snow that had swept over the route the summit rope Sherpas had fixed just nine hours before.

Tom and I hit the route, and with consistent winds of 30-40 miles per hour, we still made good time. My clear goggles froze solid from the inside within the first 30 minutes and became useless. It was of little concern, as I repeated in my mind my mantra of "I will not be denied," and the message from my daughter Ellie that I had just received on our GPS Inreach device moments before I headed out: "You got this."

With only the lights of our headlamps to guide us in the darkness of the bruised purple and black sky, the wind relentlessly struck from my left side, freezing my face and creating a small parachute with my hood. No matter how I cinched the hood drawstring, the wind would pluck it off my head. I had to manually hold the hood with one hand and hold on to the fixed line with the other. As we approached the Balcony, a ledge perched on the side of Mt. Everest at 27,700 feet, my mind focused on the small plot of snow illuminated by my headlamp, when suddenly in my periphery appeared a pair of mountaineering boots—but they were facing the wrong direction. And they were attached to a body frozen upside down to the rope from the year before. Any exhaustion I was feeling was immediately expelled from my body, replaced with laser focus. It was a sad and a stark reminder of the reality that I had entered the world's highest graveyard, and to make every step count.

When we reached the Balcony, our guides unscrewed our empty oxygen canisters and replaced them with full ones they stashed there days earlier. The two minutes it took to transition from when I was breathing bottled oxygen to the thin air of 27,700 feet, my brain felt as if it was being squeezed in a vise. All I could do was stay hunched over and wait for the rescue. With a fresh flow, we commenced our slow march, and our team was doing great. The next section is the Tenzing step, which many consider the most difficult part of the route. Since we were the first group up the mountain, except the summit rope Sherpas the previous day, Sarki wasn't sure if we were tied into the correct ropes as there were dozens of ropes to choose from—remnants of past decades of rope fixing.

However, we were now climbing vertically, and we needed to tie in, and in a hurry, so he made his best guess. While ascending,

I grabbed a basketball-sized rock that loosened and fell away. Fortunately, I was the last in our group, so it dropped harmlessly into the abyss. The hands of Pasang, one of our summit Sherpa guides, began to freeze and seize and he made it known. For a Sherpa to complain about anything, things have to be really bad.... Wind was now an indomitable foe. It pushed me back and off the mountain, as I struggled to maintain my balance while continuing to climb. Keeping my fingers moving constantly so they would not totally freeze, I set my crampon points, and ensured my ascender and carabiners were properly affixed. This became a never-ending exercise.

I continued my push toward the South Summit in horrific conditions when suddenly I saw Brandon descending my same rope toward me. "Why is he climbing down?" Few words accompany Brandon's swift communication style, and this morning was no different: "It's over, Sarki is turning us around." WHAT? The cold thin air contributed to the delay in computing what Brandon just said. "Wait!" I yelled through my mask and above the jet stream. "Let's at least hold on for the sun to rise and see if the winds will decrease." Dawn would be within an hour, and we could possibly see with better clarity what was happening just 300 feet above at the summit. Brandon explained he and Larry tried to reason with Sarki for a long time, but in the end the decision was made. It was over. Larry followed shortly behind, and I expressed the same suggestion, but Larry repeated again that they tried to convince Sarki to continue, but it was futile.

At base camp, Lhakpa had been watching the hour-to-hour forecast and keeping in radio contact with Sarki. With the ever-increasing wind speeds, only one result would happen if we continued to climb at that elevation, temperature and wind, and summiting was not the result. Sarki, a certified mountain guide with six Everest summits, knew better than we did. If we didn't want to end up like the dead climber we passed at the Balcony, we had but one choice: descend.

There was nothing more to discuss. Brandon continued to rappel down faster than I had ever seen him rappel in our seven years of climbing together. Back at home, our entire world had watched Brandon's GPS tracker stall at the South Summit. My wife was wondering if it froze, others were posting on social media assuming we had made the top since on their computer screen we were only two inches from the summit. And then Brandon's tracker dropped like a rock with his speedy descent. I stood perched on a vertical ledge in disbelief. It can't be over. It cannot be over. I tapped my helmet repeatedly against the rocks in front of me, whispering through clenched teeth: "No, no, no, this can't be it." We're at the South Summit! 300 feet from the top. The time away from family, time off work, commitment, training, preparation, risk, and the cost. This was my shot. This was our moment. And it was over.

With no alternative but to follow Sarki, I began the longest downclimb of my life. Every thought that could occupy my mind was how close I had been, and how I had failed. Whether it was from circumstances in my control or not, we had not accomplished what we had worked so long to achieve.

That day on Everest was the most difficult setback of my mountaineering life, but after recovering from the shock of having to turn around, I vowed to persist until we had achieved our goal. I learned a lot about myself during that downclimb and after, and I dedicated myself to understanding and mastering the concepts of persistence.

Throughout our lives, and no matter what our ambitions and quests, persistence can be the difference between success and failure. Persistence is why a physician, writer, or amateur athlete emerges from the millions of aspiring med students, writers, and amateur athletes to have a successful career. Persistence is why some entrepreneurs finally create the companies that revolutionize industries, even if they first fail repeatedly. And persistence is why some people have fulfilled lives, while others face years of frustration and disappointment.

This book describes how *anyone* can achieve their life's goals and ambitions, whatever they may be. For persistence is a not a quality that you either have or don't have. *Persistence can be learned and nurtured.*

In this book, you'll learn:

➢ How you must be *mentally* prepared to be persistent.

➢ How persistence in any endeavor, from climbing a mountain to graduating college, is a *physical* undertaking that requires a body in top shape.

➢ How choosing *the right people* to surround you can make the difference between failure and success.

➢ How rigorously paying attention to the *logistical details* lays the groundwork for persistence.

➤ How to become *remotivated* when you've reached your limit and want to abandon your goal.

➤ How to avoid *the dark side* of persistence, when persistence transforms into foolish and dangerous obstinance.

Peak Persistence is filled with tales of mountain climbing adventures, including personal experiences on the world's highest summits, inspiring stories and examples of people who overcame insurmountable odds to succeed in a wide variety of domains, and academic research that explains and supports how-to steps for acquiring and sustaining persistence.

This is a book about triumph and tragedy on the world's highest peaks as well as the summits and valleys of life. "Our greatest success is just one step beyond our greatest failure," said Napoleon Hill. *Peak Persistence* looks at what happens when you take one step beyond. One step into the unknown. Into risk, into discomfort. It explores what happens when your climb doesn't go as planned. And why some persist and reach life's greatest summits while others turn back.

PART ONE

WHY PERSIST?

CHAPTER ONE

NO SUMMIT WITHOUT PERSISTENCE

I will persist until I succeed. Always will I take another step. If that is of no avail, I will take another, and yet another. In truth, one step at a time is not too difficult. I know that small attempts, repeated, will complete any undertaking.

— Og Mandino

Standing at an altitude of 22,841 feet, Mt. Aconcagua is the highest peak in the world outside of the Himalayas. Five years before our failed attempt on Everest, Tom, Larry, Brandon and I, along with three additional friends, attempted to reach the summit of Aconcagua in January 2012. I was among four of our group of seven to reach the top, but I'm still not sure how. I have never felt as sick and weak on any mountain as I felt on January 11, 2012, when the weather finally cleared enough for us to attempt the summit.

Two weeks of climbing led to our arrival at our final high camp, Camp Colera. At an elevation of 19,258 feet, Camp Colera is a fairly flat, rocky area large enough for a dozen tents and the platform from which all expeditions stage for their summit push. The edge of the camp looks over a 3,000-foot drop; exposed on the north ridge, the camp leaves no protection from the wind.

Witnessing gusts of wind so strong they had flung an unoccupied tent off this platform, Larry and Brandon had to sprawl flat on my tent while Tom and I speared poles up the sleeves and roped guy lines around rocks to keep our tent from taking a 3,000-foot flight. During the night, sleep was near impossible with the constant flapping of the tent walls and hoarfrost raining from above. I never managed to sleep longer than a half hour without waking. I continually checked my watch, futilely hoping that more time had passed and that I had managed just a little more sleep. Finally, after 36 hours, counting the interior fabric lines of the tent waiting out the wind and snow flurries, we had a window to head for the summit. It was 3:30 a.m., and we began our preparations. After a lengthy two hours of getting ready, we prayed as a group for protection and safe return, and "Team Chupacabra" was on its way.

With my first steps from Camp Colera, I knew I was in trouble. I had zero energy. Several weeks at crushing altitude, insufficient water and possible dehydration, and subsisting on nothing but freeze-dried meals that had long since lost their appeal had completely drained me of all energy reserves. As I began climbing higher, each step added to the sensation that my legs were filled with concrete. No matter how fatigued I'd been on other climbs, this was my first encounter with struggling just to put one step in front of the other and take one step higher up the mountain. To compound the matter, about an hour into the summit bid, diarrhea kicked in and sapped any reserves I may have had left. Annoyingly, my compression shirt kept rolling up, cutting into my mid-section and exerting pressure. In negative 0-degree temperatures and high winds, I took off my shirt, moved a few feet off the route, and did my business for all the slowing ascending climbers to witness. Brandon also had a similar situation and joined me. Cheek to cheek, we found humor in our humiliation. Grateful to have someone to laugh with, I put back on my layers, and we continued.

Describing the experience as miserable wouldn't even begin to do justice to how it felt. It was at about that time that our highly experienced Argentinian guide, Juani, decided to turn Larry around due to his pace. In Larry's early climbing days, his determination outperformed his experience at altitude, and, while he was always willing, his body was not. Now when we climb, Larry understands his high-altitude physiology and crushes the peaks he attempts. Our group of seven original climbers that had started at high camp was now down to four.

Jaime, another climbing guide we had specifically hired only for the summit day, escorted Larry down to high camp then came back quickly and re-joined us. Jaime's speed in taking Larry down and then catching back to us was undeniably incredible, yet demoralizing. Here I am pulling from everything I have just to take one more step, and Jaime comes cruising by *like he's out for a Sunday stroll in the park.* As for me, I would drag myself a few steps, lean over to rest on my climbing axe and repeat—over and over, again and again. My mind was clear—believe me I knew exactly where I was with each painful step and effort—and my lungs were fine, but my legs had been replaced with useless cement stumps. Somehow, I moved forward until we reached a resting point at an emergency hut called Indepencia. I laid flat on my side and proceeded to vomit four separate times. I managed to get my hood out of my vomit path the first three times, but on the fourth I wasn't so lucky. Tom, a true friend who, full of compassion, cared about my welfare while struggling with his own crushing fatigue, brushed the mixture of vomit and snow away from my face as I lay there trying to fleck off the frozen regurgitated orange Gatorade. Tom and Brandon later commented that as they shone their headlamps on my face, it was an ashen gray that they had never seen before nor knew could happen to someone's skin color.

Lying there, feeble as a newborn baby, I was at the end of the line. But Juani came over and asked me: "How is your head? How are your lungs?" Juani knew the proper way to assess the signs of cerebral and pulmonary edema, or fluid buildup around the brain and lungs. I said I was okay. He paused only for a moment and returned with, "I think you can do it," and went on to check my other friends. And so, I took Juani's word for it and continued, stopping and slumping over my axe every few steps, just long enough to regain the ability and composure to take a few more.

This process repeated for two hours until we arrived at the base of "the Traverse." Staring at me was a long vertical traverse across a broad snowfield that I would have to cross before reaching "the Cave." I was still feeling horrible and only getting worse. I took that moment to reflect on everything that had gotten me here, the fumes that I was pulling from just to make it this far and realized a hard truth: I could no longer continue. All the preparation, team leadership, logistics, cost, time away from my family—and I had to abandon the climb. This realization devastated me, but I knew the hours ahead in this altitude were impossible in my condition. I informed Juani that this was the end of the line, and I could go no further. Stubbornly, Juani asked again, "How is your mind? How are your lungs?" I responded as I did before. He took a moment to search my eyes, and again with total confidence and reassurance, he said, "I think you can do it"— and before I could protest or give much of an argument, we started across the Traverse. Slowly, methodically, we moved along. Jaime encouraged me to move slower and to breathe—he demonstrated by inhaling through his nose and pressure breathing through his mouth. This was a very effective exercise that helped me not think of the monumental task still ahead and to stay focused on only following the next breath and the next step.

The Traverse was a long stretch across a snowfield that seemed to cover the width of the upper mountain. The most aggressive and difficult section was right before the Cave. Somehow, we reached the Cave, where I promptly collapsed and immediately fell into a semi-conscious slumber. In that indistinct space between sleep and consciousness, I could hear Jaime speaking to Juani, and I understood enough Spanish to know that Jaime was telling Juani I needed to descend. A few moments later, Juani woke me and determined it would be good for me to now go down. I had started snoring, so I think that had a lot to do with what he suggested—I had slipped into a deep sleep within seconds in a freezing, exposed landscape, which is not an easy thing to do, and not a good sign. He said that I needed to think of my family and to think of my health. I told him I agreed and respected his decision. He then asked for the third time about my head and lungs, which once again I said were fine (which was why my complete fatigue was so frustrating!). He reminded me that we were still two more hours from the summit. He again assessed my condition by looking into my eyes while monitoring my breathing and pallor; and after a longer pause, his reply from the previous two times of "I think you can do it" changed: "Okay, I *know* you can do it." I'm still not sure what changed his decision; he had agreed with Jaime to send me down, yet now he saw something that no one else could see. I guess having the experience of guiding so many others up this mountain, he made the determination that I had the fortitude to do it.

I left my backpack to shed as much weight as possible at the Cave, as it was unneeded for the final push to the summit and, decidedly lighter, continued onward. I plodded along. Thirty minutes passed and then an hour and then two hours. I didn't stop. We just kept going. Until we could go no higher. It's difficult to explain how I ultimately summitted, how I was able to advance for two hours with nothing supporting my body, but there I was, on the rooftop of the Andes Mountains—the highest point on earth outside the Himalayas.

I said many a prayer and continued to shake my head in disbelief of how I was where I was. Tears from exhaustion and the success of the summit filled my eyes. Exulting in the company of my team, I snapped a few photos. Altogether, we spent a total of 15 minutes on the top before heading down. I collected a dozen rocks from the summit, some of which I later presented as a gift to our group. Collecting a rock from the top has been a habit on any significant peak I'm fortunate enough to reach.

On the way down, we saw our new friend Peter, a biology professor at Boston University. It was good to see him and his group only a few hundred feet from the summit. It wasn't until several days later that we learned the Aconcagua climbing rangers turned them around just minutes from the summit due to the weather that was quickly closing in; they never got the opportunity to finish their summit bid. Another example of how, in mountain climbing, just a few minutes can make all the difference in the world.

As we traveled down, our group was enveloped in a whiteout, but fortunately our experienced guides led us safely down. Once back in Camp Colera at around 6 p.m., Tom and I collapsed into our bags, hungry, thirsty, dehydrated, and lacking any and all motivation to move. We ignored trying to boil water and eating. Instead, we fell asleep and slept for 14 hours.

I had done almost everything right preparing for Aconcagua. I had trained hard, I had the right equipment and supplies, I had my trusted group around me, and an experienced guide. But I never would have made the summit without the quiet reassurance and persistence of Juani telling me unequivocally, "I know you can do it." I trusted him, and although my body was saying something completely different, those six words were all I needed to persist and reach the summit.

Sometimes the line between persistence and retreat can be very thin indeed.

Had I descended without summiting, I have no doubt that would have been my last climb of a big mountain. The quest to reach the Seven Summits would have ended right where I would have turned back—and I tried to turn back on three different occasions.

Earlier in the expedition, I wrote, "This pain and voluntary discomfort is ridiculous, and I am never doing this again." At that time, the struggle, the pain, the commitment, and the time for a summit was simply, in my mind, not worth it. Going home without a summit would have solidified that feeling. Climbing is so much more than the summit, but for me on that mountain that day, it wasn't. It wouldn't have led to the other summits I eventually planned the following years. It wouldn't have opened the door to the adventure companies I founded, the relationships, the networking opportunities, and the opportunities to be, as it turned out, the leader who has put together each of our seven summit expeditions. And if I didn't have a guide who knew me better than I knew my own abilities, I wouldn't be leading the life and lifestyle I enjoy today. I owe a great deal of what I am and have today to the belief Juani had that I could continue.

ENTREPRENEURIAL DESPAIR

Although I have a day job, I'm also an entrepreneur who has started a number of different ventures and businesses. And in my entrepreneurial life, I've had those moments when I felt like I did on the horrible climb up Aconcagua: "This is it; I cannot continue." Only there was even more—much more—at stake.

And it took a special moment with my daughter for me to realize that I *had* to start believing in myself.

In 2006, my business partner and I started several businesses. One was purchasing a spine rehabilitation franchise; another was forming a residential and commercial real estate lending fund. We found our medical office location, designed and built out all the necessary rooms for our patients, hired medically trained staff, and opened our doors. At the same time, we began funding our lending business primarily with my partner's and my personal money. As the doors opened, we began to see a steady stream of new patients.

And the real estate projects were also going well. One lot of land we purchased for $80,000 and sold for $140,000 within two weeks. Returns were high, and money was easy.

And then the avalanche broke loose. In April of 2007, a commercial construction project we had heavily invested in went bankrupt. We were under the impression that we held first position on the property and might be able to recoup some of our investment. Unfortunately, we discovered we had been lied to, and my business partner and I lost all of our $90,000 in our second position. We had also invested in the Avanti Capital Investment fund, which the Security and Exchange Commission later discovered was using investor funds to make interest payments. The interest payments slowly stopped coming, and our efforts to communicate with the owner went unanswered. This company slowly went under, and all our invested money was gone.

There was more.

In a speculative home that we built for resale, somehow the builder thought a salmon pink stucco exterior would be a nice choice. This new home never even got a single look—or if it did, it was a look of disgust. We had to sink further funds to quickly paint the exterior. We took a substantial loss to sell it so as to forgo making additional mortgage payments.

Another project of apartments we invested in was highly leveraged, and a mortgage on that property failed, along with all our capital.

The final blow was when the spine rehabilitation franchises also failed and took with it our $75,000 franchise fee. Neither we nor the other four franchisee owners across the state could bear the $35,000 per month operating costs to keep the doors open, and one by one each franchise owner filed for bankruptcy. Except for our location. While we did close the doors, my business partner maintained his obligations and never did file for bankruptcy.

At this point, we had three young children, and I was the sole provider for my family as my wife was a full-time stay at home mom.

My wife and I had worked hard, saved everything, tried to make the right financial choices (such as eating a lot of ramen noodles!) so that by 29 years old we were completely debt-free and nearly owning our home outright.

Now at 30, I was worse than broke. Within six months, our entire savings, all our assets—the business holdings as well as all the $240,000 equity in my home, which I foolishly leveraged to purchase more investments—were gone. I started from nothing and was now below nothing after a decade of earning and investing and finally reaching a position to be proud of. Not only were we totally broke, I also had to come up with a $980 interest-only loan payment that I was on the hook from the $240,000 home equity line of credit. Since it was interest only, that payment wouldn't put a dent in the loan balance. I didn't see how I would ever get out from under this debt load. Each morning I would wake up with what felt like a pushpin in the lower half of my stomach.

My commission-only job in commercial real estate during the bust of 2007 made our income uncertainty a certainty. We were going backward each month.

Finally, I had my rock-bottom moment. My three daughters were five, three, and one at the time. One morning, my middle daughter was eating a bowl of cereal next to me on the barstool. As she looked up at me with a big smile, milk dripping down her chin, I began weeping, not knowing where her next bowl of cereal would come from. I had to turn away and leave the room. I went into our little laundry room and just covered my face and wept.

It's unbelievable to think about it now, with a rational mind, but had I had a quick means to do so, I very well could have made a permanent decision to address a temporary problem. Because it was at this dark moment that my State Farm agent called to verify some policy information, and I asked him, in a nonchalant way, what happens with life insurance policies if someone commits suicide. He told me that if the policy has been active for over two years (which mine had been) then it would pay out. I felt the real possibility that I was better off dead. I felt if my family only had a few hundred thousand dollars, that could cover my mistakes.

The turning point came one Saturday morning when I set out to do a Daddy-daughter date. We went to make paper boats and float them down a nearby irrigation stream. As I watched my daughter place her simple, barely floating boat into the water and it was whisked down the stream, somehow my thoughts of ending my life went with it. I was overcome with a sense of reassurance that it would work out in the end. My inner thought continued: if it hasn't worked out yet, it's not the end. I made a silent promise to myself, my daughters, and my wife that I would never put myself or them in this position again. Before, I blamed others— thinking of how the spine clinic franchise owners had created a flawed company and wasted our money, how the contractor had chosen a ridiculous pink stucco, how several of our real estate holdings were purchased by fraudulent investors— but in reality, it was my fault. No one prevented me from doing our due diligence on an unproven franchise. No colorblind contractor made me neglect a spec home we were building. No economy slump had forced me to invest in poor properties. I was in this position because of one person.

The next morning, with the image of the stream and my smiling daughter in my mind, I went into my office with a newfound determination and energy. I worked hard and began to focus on what other strengths I had accumulated in the few years of my twenties that I could translate into value as a product or service. I have always been in sales, and so I knew I could sell, but could there be a possibility of starting a business related to my skill set or area of expertise and do it better than the current competitors?

LAUNCHING MY ADVENTURE COMPANIES

There's nothing quite like desperation to serve as motivation. After the collapse of our finances, I was continually running the math of our future in every possible way I could think of. I soon realized that unless I took one step beyond in every area of my life, we would continue to sink further and further into financial ruin.

In 2008, I climbed a small mountain in Mexico called Orizaba. We booked the trip through a locally-owned business run by the Canchola family. The Cancholas are a humble, hard-working family who have been running a climbing operation for decades but have no online presence. After the climb, my friend mentioned that it might be a good idea to create a website and help them with inquiries and marketing. A few hurdles quickly became apparent. I didn't speak Spanish. I didn't know how to build a website. I didn't know how to do any form of online marketing. But I decided to not let any of these things stop me.

Back home, I found someone who knew how to build websites and paid a nominal fee to create a very simple site. I started handling inquiries from potential clients and created a packet with logistical information to send once they booked. I became familiar with Google Translate and found the most effective ways to communicate with the Canchola family (who do not speak English). Within one season, we had tripled their client volume, and the Cancholas were elated with the results.

The following year, when my cousin-in-law asked if I might be interested in climbing the Matterhorn, I said yes, but upon further inspection of the technical climbing requirements, he got cold feet and we set on climbing Kilimanjaro in Africa instead. I was really intrigued but had no idea how I would afford it. An oft repeated phrase in our house by Zig Zigler is: "You can have everything in life you want, if you will just help other people get what they want." I put the word out and assembled our group of nine to climb Kilimanjaro and safari and built in my costs to cover my travel. I started researching guide companies and tried to find local guides that were a lot further down the Google rabbit hole and which, in turn, would be a lot cheaper. Through my research, a light bulb idea started to form. What if I could replicate the same business model I had used for Orizaba and find a local operator who was savvy on the mountain but not so savvy in the online marketplace? With that in mind, I registered Climbkili.com. Now all I needed was a trustworthy local partner to take care of ground operations, and I could figure out everything else. I sent out emails to dozens of local operators, four of which responded and three of which agreed to meet with me when I arrived in Tanzania. I came prepared with beanies and shirts adorned with the new logo I had created. I knew this was my one shot for pictures and future marketing material, so I took a chance and hoped it would pan out.

Nickson Moshi was by far the most impressive guide with his presentation, confidence, and business savvy mindset. He came to our meeting with half a dozen staff members who demonstrated setting up tents, setting up stove equipment and tables they use on the mountain, and explaining to me the ins and outs of how they run a climb. This was extremely impressive because I had just gotten off the mountain with a team that was using inferior equipment, food, and products. I got the sense right away that

Nickson was a man who cared about the details, took pride in his team and would take excellent care of our future clients. His team respected him, and he showed that same respect to them. I told him of my plans to form a business, and he agreed to be a part of it. We formed a loose partnership neither of us quite trusting the other, not quite sure how each other would fit within the business, but both knowing we needed each other to make this international adventure company successful. One great quality about Nickson is his endless optimism. Before I left Tanzania, he smiled and with excitement in his voice said, "We are going to be the best company on Kili." I was a little more skeptical but hoped for the best.

We were broke. To build a website costs thousands, and we barely had a few hundred. I was able to negotiate with a friend who built our first website to take a side job for $700. I remember calculating and telling a friend I would be elated if we could book four clients a month. That would cover my car payment, our second mortgage and a little bit of our first mortgage—and in so doing, allow me to breathe for the first time in three years. With Nickson's help we acquired photos of our new team wearing our gear, graphics of the routes, testimonials from clients who had gone with his crew, and launched our website. With no knowledge of search engine optimization or how to rank in Google, I spent my free time doing my homework. I attended SEO classes at night, published online articles, and optimized the back end of the website where Google crawls to provide searchers the right results. My wife worked on formalized itineraries, communicated with clients, and formed relationships with the office staff in Africa.

Little by little, we developed protocols and procedures that would ensure client satisfaction and summit success.

We hung out in online forums where potential clients would research Kilimanjaro tour companies and found any and every way to market. Within our first year, we had booked 30 clients, which we were thrilled with. The next year, we jumped to 200 new bookings, which was a dream come true. We felt like we had made it! The following year gained momentum like a freight train, and we reached an astounding 600 new client bookings. Since that year, we've never been at less than 600 new bookings. We have grown our staff both in Tanzania and the U.S. to employ more than 200 people on a consistent basis. Within a few years, we were also able to expand into the safari business, developing a thriving safari company and building a luxury tented camp in the Serengeti where our clients can relax.

All of this happened while I was working a full-time job.

In the depths of our financial problems, I had considered the ultimate act of giving up. But I persisted, first by making the decision to refuse to give up, and then by looking for solutions to move forward. Starting any company is a risk. Starting one when you're broke is even riskier. But I have always had an entrepreneurial spirit, and I persisted in entrepreneurship until I had founded two companies focused on what I love doing the most: climbing mountains and discovering new adventures.

WHAT MOTIVATES PERSISTENCE? LESSONS FROM ENTREPRENEURSHIP

This determination to persist in the face of failure or even after failure is a recurring theme of successful lives in careers and endeavors where rejection and failure are ubiquitous. Entrepreneurship, for example, is a domain where failure has the dominant win record. Few entrepreneurs have succeeded without failure, but failure only inspires the successful entrepreneurs to keep trying even harder.

I love our Dyson products. My wife blow-dries her hair with a Dyson, we have a handheld vacuum for our kitchen and two upright vacuums for our house. We could get away with one vacuum, but I'm so impressed with this company and their innovations that we enjoy having several iterations of their evolving technology.

The inventor of the Dyson vacuum cleaner and the founder of the company, James Dyson, is a billionaire. He persisted with his idea against insurmountable odds to achieve peak success.

Dyson's idea came to him not out of a creative search, but from a completely unplanned source: frustration with housecleaning. He hated vacuum cleaners. He hated them as a kid and hated them as an adult. Because he hated working with the vacuum bags. And one day in 1979, the industrial engineer was doing household chores alongside his wife Dierdre when he had to empty a vacuum cleaner bag; he couldn't replace the bag because he did not have any replacements. That was the final straw. "With this lifelong hatred of the way the machine worked, I decided to make a bagless vacuum cleaner," he said.

Sometimes you have to get great at the things you hate.

For the next five years, Dyson would develop 5,127 prototypes of a vacuum cleaner that would use centrifugal force to pick up dust and spin it into a canister. During that time, he says, "I was getting further and further into debt. Thankfully, my wife was very supportive. Bankruptcy didn't worry me because I can make things, but I did worry about losing our house. My wife sold paintings and taught art classes, and we borrowed, and borrowed, and borrowed. We grew our own vegetables, and she made clothes for the children."

Once the new vacuum cleaner was developed, Dyson set out to look for manufacturers. All the major appliance manufacturers rejected him for one reason or another, until he finally found a small Japanese company named Apex to produce the new machine. Sales were poor as Apex marketed the machine as a very expensive ($2,000) niche product. So, in the early 1990s, Dyson decided to manufacture the vacuum cleaners himself.

"None of the venture capitalists and banks would lend me money until 1993, when my bank manager, Mike Page, personally lobbied Lloyds Bank to lend me the money I needed for tooling." Now manufacturing his invention, Dyson found a mail-order company willing to list it. Eventually other mail-order companies accepted the product, and within two years, the Dyson vacuum cleaner was the best-selling vacuum in the U.K. In 2002, nearly 25 years after that fateful day of housecleaning, Best Buy in the U.S. agreed to start selling his vacuum cleaner in the United States.

Today, Dyson machines, including vacuums, hair dryers, and air treatment machines, are sold in 65 countries and the one-man Dyson company is now a global technology company with more than 1,000 engineers. And because of Dyson's continued commitment to serve and innovate, he was in a position during the COVID-19 pandemic, to develop—in 10 days—a completely new ventilator called the CoVent. "A ventilator supports a patient who is no longer able to maintain their own airways. This new device can be manufactured quickly, efficiently and at volume" said Dyson. His persistent determination to fix a dusty vacuum bag long ago, has now led in saving tens of thousands of lives.

BEFORE THEY WERE FAMOUS: BELIEVING IN YOURSELF

Believing in yourself is the engine of persistence. It's where it all begins. I remember as a kid loving the training montage of Rocky IV. Cold, destitute in some remote cabin in the U.S.S.R., and having to train to fight a giant against all odds. It's a scene I pull up on YouTube when I need a little nostalgic training inspiration before my own mountain workouts. But there would be no Rocky IV (or Forty—whatever the number's up to now) if Sylvester Stallone didn't persist when there was an easier way out.

When Sylvester Stallone was writing the script for the movie, *Rocky*, he could not have known just how closely fiction would mirror fact. Like Rocky at the beginning of the movie, Sylvester

Stallone was a nobody, a struggling actor among an ocean of other actors trying to make it in Hollywood. He had a little bit of success in a New York movie called *The Lords of Flatbush* and had decided to move to California to become a Hollywood movie star. Instead, he found himself so poor that he had to sell his "best friend, his confidant"—his pet dog Butkus—for $40 in front of a 7-Eleven just to pay the bills.

One night he saw Chuck Wepner, a journeyman boxer known as the Bayonne Bleeder, fight the greatest boxer of all time, Muhammed Ali. And Wepner actually lasted through 15 rounds of the fight and even knocked down Ali.

The fight he witnessed inspired Stallone to whip out a script in three months about a boxer fighting the champ and against all odds becoming victorious. As he was writing, he continued to plug away at auditions, always waiting for his break.

At one audition, he was yet again rejected, not being "right for the role." By that time, his script was finished and tucked away in his apartment. As he left the audition, he mentioned to the producers the story he had written. They were interested in seeing it.

He brought them the script, and before he knew it, they wanted to turn it into a movie. He was still dirt poor, having $106 in his bank account. They offered $360,000 for the script. Imagine being so poor you sell your best friend, and suddenly you're offered $360,000. Would you take it?

Stallone said, no thanks. Because part of the deal was that a Hollywood star would play the Rocky role, and Stallone was no star. He wasn't even a working actor. And Stallone wanted to play the role.

So, he walked away from $360,000. When the producers realized that Stallone was not giving up, they relented and gave him $1 million to make the movie. Even though this was 1977, $1 million was barely enough to make a feature film. Stallone used friends and family, filmed the movie in his city, Philadelphia, and the rest, as they say, is movie history.

But only because of Sylvester Stallone's amazing persistence in trying to be an actor. He finally gets a movie in New York, moves to LA, makes no money, but when he hits what many would consider a jackpot, he realizes that what he wants is *to be an actor.*

I don't think Sylvester Stallone is the world's greatest actor. I would bet you that there are thousands and thousands of supremely talented actors who have trekked to Hollywood and failed. Because they didn't have the kind of persistence and internal strength that Stallone showed in turning down almost four hundred grand so he could do what he wanted to do. (And by the way, he was also able to buy his dog back… after agreeing to let the new owner be in the movie!)

The story of Harry Potter author J.K. Rowling is another great story of the rewards of persistence. While her struggles as a welfare mom writing on the subway and in cafés are well-known, few people realize that Rowling had been writing stories all her life—even as a child. Rowling didn't pen Harry Potter to get out of debt, she penned Harry Potter because all she ever wanted to do in life was to tell stories. Her parents, who had been very poor, insisted that she could not make a living as a writer. As she recalls in her famous Harvard commencement speech:

I was convinced that the only thing I wanted to do, ever, was to write novels. However, my parents, both of whom came from impoverished backgrounds and neither of whom had been to college, took the view that my overactive imagination was an amusing personal quirk that would never pay a mortgage, or secure a pension.

While her parents wanted her to take a vocational degree that would set her up for a career in a trade, Rowling instead went to college to study perhaps the most useless subject in terms of careers: classics. Seven years after graduating, Rowling continues in her Harvard address,

I had failed on an epic scale. An exceptionally short-lived marriage had imploded, and I was jobless, a lone parent, and as poor as it is possible to be in modern Britain, without being homeless. The fears that my parents had had for me, and that I had had for myself, had both come to pass, and by every usual standard, I was the biggest failure I knew.

Ironically, that failure motivated Rowling to persist even more at becoming a novelist. "I stopped pretending to myself that I was anything other than what I was, and began to direct all my energy into finishing the only work that mattered to me," she told the Harvard graduates. "I was set free, because my greatest fear had been realized, and I was still alive, and I still had a daughter whom I adored, and I had an old typewriter and a big idea. And so rock bottom became the solid foundation on which I rebuilt my life."

Many people give up in the face of failure. If your entire success is based solely on reaching the summit, you're going to miss all that comes with the beauty of the journey. The story of J.K. Rowling is telling because failure, in her case, had the exact opposite impact on her: it made her more determined to persist than ever.

TENACITY OVER TALENT: LARDOG THE CONQUEROR

If you're thinking to yourself, "I don't have the talent to write bestselling novels, I don't have the brawn to become an action film star, I don't have this or that..."

Persistence doesn't come from what you have. It comes from what you *believe* and what you *want*.

If you saw my friend Larry Daugherty walking on the street, you would never believe the adventures that this guy has accomplished. He's not very big physically. He has an infectious laugh. He has a brilliant mind and leads a thriving career as a radiation oncologist.

He also wants to be the first person to climb Mt. Everest and run the Iditarod in the same year. Obviously for most people, either one of those would be once-in-a-lifetime accomplishments. Larry wants to achieve both within a few months of each other. And I have no doubt he will do it one day.

Because when Larry decides to do something, he never gives up until it happens. For many years, Larry would tell his friends that someday he would run the Iditarod, the great dog sled race across Alaska. Even when he was an oncologist working at the Mayo Clinic in Jacksonville, Florida—about as far from Alaska as you can get and still be in the U.S.—he insisted that someday his dream would come true. He even told his future wife on their first date about the Iditarod dream. He had never even been on a dog sled, but that didn't matter.

One day, on a flight from Europe, he saw an ad in *Outside* magazine about a dogsled race in the arctic reaches of Norway, and when he got home, he talked to his wife about it and signed up that very night. The Fjallraven Polar only accepts a few individuals from a handful of countries; to be able to enter, Larry's entry video would have to garner the most votes in a contest. Larry persisted, and it paid off: he won by a nose.

Mushing—driving the dog sleds—turned out to be everything he had dreamt about. After the Fjallraven Polar, Larry was more determined than ever to race the Iditarod. He had a good life in the warm, flat lands of Florida, including a job he loved at a prestigious hospital, but when he saw an ad for a radiation oncologist in Alaska, he knew this was his chance. He moved his family the 4,640 miles from Jacksonville to Anchorage, started participating in qualifying races, and finally in 2016, his dream came true. He qualified for the Iditarod!

One day, there was Larry on the famed Iditarod trail, and he was so excited that in the midst of the race he lost track of where he was… and got lost! As he explains it, the Iditarod course consists of the main trail and little side trails that you can take for a short time before they swing back into the main trail. Larry took one of the side trails, not realizing that he was in fact turning off the course and heading in a completely different direction! Adding to the confusion was that the Junior Iditarod had taken the trail that Larry was just on, and so he was seeing Iditarod markers (not noticing that they said "Iditarod Junior") and the dog poop from the previous race. So he had no idea that anything was wrong...until he hit the Yetna River. That's when he knew instantly that he had made a major mistake, that he had been following the wrong path for several hours: the Yetna River was some 40 miles away from the course. It wasn't just a matter of retracing his steps. By the time he got back on the course, he would have run an extra 60 miles with no feed stations and supplies along the way. Mushers re-supply at pre-determined "checkpoints," where drop bags prepared weeks before are waiting. Larry had missed the checkpoint and was now nearly half a day from the next one. He looked at the food he had with him and decided to try to make it to the next stop from where he was, ignoring his only other choice: going back to the now closer prior checkpoint, but risking withdrawal from the race due to no longer being competitive.

By carefully rationing supplies, he was somehow able to make it to the next checkpoint, then the next, and ultimately finish the race. He would go down in history as one of the Lost Boys, running the longest Iditarod in history.

In 2017, Larry made his first attempt at doing what had now become his second dream: to become the first person to run the Iditarod and climb Mt. Everest in the same year. He finished 44th in the Iditarod and was by my side when we were 300 feet from the summit of Everest.

Larry's persistence in making his incredible dream of running the Iditarod come true (he's now done it four times) convinces me that whatever he wants to do, he will be able to do it—even if no human has done it before. In 2020 Larry set out for his second attempt at 'Iditarest' (Larry's coined term for Iditarod and Everest) was again tragically cut short due to the Nepali government canceling the Everest climbing season for 2020 due to COVID-19. I'm convinced he will succeed one day. Lardog, as I affectionately call him, is the very definition of persistence.

NO SUMMIT TOO HIGH WITH PERSISTENCE

Stephen Hawking. Simply saying the name of this famously brilliant, and equally famously disabled, physicist is enough to underscore the lesson of this section: with persistence, anything is possible.

Another example of overcoming the odds is the incredible story of someone in my field of endeavor: mountain climbing. Erik Weihenmayer has reached the Seven Summits, which is a difficult achievement for any human being. But imagine climbing the highest peaks on all seven continents when you are *blind*. This is the feat accomplished by Weihenmayer.

When he was just four years old, Weihenmayer was diagnosed with retinoschisis, which is a disease that progressively causes you to lose your sight. Weihenmayer was completely blind by the time he was 14. At first he rebelled, refusing to learn braille or use a cane, and ended up falling down the stairs. Then he changed his attitude and decided that being blind was not going to stop him from doing anything he wanted. And he discovered that what he wanted to do was rock climbing. As he told an interviewer in 2018, "Shortly after going blind, I received a newsletter in Braille about a group taking blind kids rock climbing. I thought to myself, 'Who would be crazy enough to take a blind kid rock climbing?' So I signed up!"

Once a month, his father would drive him from their home in Connecticut to an adventure program for the blind in Massachusetts. Rock climbing became his passion. When he graduated from college, he moved to Arizona, where he joined the Arizona Mountaineering Club. Finally in 2001, he decided to attempt to scale the mountain that had first introduced me to mountaineering, Mt. Rainier in Washington. After conquering Rainier, he set his sights on Kilimanjaro. My Kilimanjaro business partner, Nickson, would be his guide to the top on one of his Kilimanjaro summits. The challenges for a blind mountaineer are screamingly obvious. On a big mountain, Erik follows the sounds of his climbing partners' crampons in the snow. When he's on a rock, his partners are jingling a bear bell, which keeps him from the edge, and he's also using two trekking poles to feel his way. As for an ice face, Erik uses his rock climbing skills, feeling his way with his hands.

But even the simplest things can be a challenge when you're blind. When climbing a significant mountain, most mountaineers are accustomed to using a pee bottle inside your tent. That's life on the mountain. One day, during his Aconcagua climb, Erik mistook a pee bottle for his water bottle. Lesson learned. The two bottles were clearly marked in different ways from then on.

Climbing the Seven Summits with sight requires an immense amount of persistence through years of trials and setbacks. You have to multiply that by 100 if you're blind. I was proud that my business partner guided Erik to achieve his second of his seven summits. Especially since Kilimanjaro has a special significance for him. As he explains on his website, he married his wife, Ellie, on his first expedition up the mountain. And on his expedition with Nickson, he led a team of both blind and sighted climbers from four continents, including Douglas Sidialo, a Nigerian blinded in the 1998 U.S. embassy bombing who, like Erik, refuses to let his blindness stop him from a life of adventures and triumphs.

Weihenmayer is one of the greatest examples of the power of persistence.

PART TWO

THE FOUNDATIONS OF
PERSISTENCE

CHAPTER TWO

THE MOUNTAIN MINDSET: YOU GET WHAT YOU DEMAND, NOT WHAT YOU EXPECT

What lies behind us and what lies before us are small matters compared to what lies within us.

— Henry Haskins

6:20 a.m., Day 14, Denali: The sun rose majestically over a low, snow-capped ridge, my lungs teased the atmosphere with short, crisp exhalations, leaving vapor meandering in the frigid air… Just kidding! Alaska, in the summer, offers 24 hours of light, so you can climb at any time of the day or night. It's one of the few advantages and breaks you get when climbing Denali. I never experienced a sunrise, nor sunset, for that matter, while climbing the highest and one of the most challenging peaks in North America. For two solid weeks we'd been working our way steadfastly up the mountain, repeatedly pulling 70-pound sleds of gear across powder-covered snowfields, through technical ice sections, and over tenuous crevasse crossings. Denali doesn't easily bend to anyone's will, and our team's experience was no exception. We literally moved at a glacial pace up the mountain, marking our progress in feet not miles. All the while battling the notoriously formidable Denali weather. After climbing and waiting, climbing and waiting again for two solid weeks, we prayed for my wife to text us some good news—that the winds were finally dying down, and there was the remotest possibility of a summit window. With relief, she texted that the forecast predicted the impassable conditions on the peak would finally break, making a summit attempt possible; we didn't hesitate: we loaded our gear and headed out of Camp 14, named for its position at 14,000 feet. It was Monday, and the window to summit appeared to open only briefly, on Tuesday or Wednesday. Apparently, the rest of the mountain had received the same news. With a perfect view of the Headwall (an 800-foot near-vertical section of ice separating our camp from the final High Camp), I counted, at one time, 60 climbers all heading up to the same section of one fixed rope for ascension.

Our team was comprised of two rope teams, which I'll refer to as Salt Lake and Seattle because that's where each of the teams originated. As usual, Brandon was prepared to go long before the rest of us, which gave us a head start on our three Seattle teammates. With Brandon in the lead, me in the middle, and Tom anchoring the end, we roped up and let team Seattle know we were underway. It appeared they would be maybe 15 minutes behind us; we'd stay in contact with them through our radios. Wishing them a good climb, we departed from camp and made quick progress to the base of the Headwall. Upon arrival, dishearteningly, I counted now 80 climbers ahead of us, and we recognized that we were among the last to leave camp.

Most climbers make a preliminary climb up the Headwall and leave a cache of supplies for everything needed for their High

Camp, as a summit attempt is too difficult carrying all the necessary gear and supplies in one heavy vertical haul. Such a climb also provides an opportunity to acclimatize, stretch the legs, make use of the better weather lower on the mountain, and makes for a lighter load when your group decides to head up to the final High Camp for good. This, at least, is the philosophy of the professionally guided groups. As for our own group, we decided to pack the minimum: three days of food with the intent to do a single carry and only one trip up the Headwall. If we didn't have a summit window by then, well, we gave it our best (this technique is something I have used on multiple summits around the world, and it has been successful for my team). There's a careful balancing act between exerting too much energy with extra trips up the mountain and risking too few supplies if you have to wait out weather. We err on the side of fast and efficient.

As a side note, just days before, our neighboring "Minnesota" climbers—two men in their 50's—came back to camp ushered by the Denali Climbing Rangers. The Rangers were making sure one of them, "Pete," was packing his gear and heading off the mountain. It turns out "Pete" was hauling gear up the Headwall and was growing impatient with the climber in front of him. His impatience overrode his common sense, to the point that he felt the need to unclip his safety device from the rope and free climb a 70-degree ice face to bypass this climber. An insanely risky move. "Pete" made it about two steps before his steel crampon points bounced off the bulletproof ice, sending him hurtling in an uncontrollable freefall down the face. An alert climber, who was tied into the rope, saw this unfold and swung over to catch the now-cascading Pete, saving him from certain injury or death. Trying to climb the Headwall without being clipped in was a reckless, irresponsible, and foolish choice that ended his (and his blameless climbing partner's) climb and almost his life. When we heard his story, we expressed our gratitude for his safe return and condolences for having to descend without a chance at the summit—although there is no doubt that the Rangers made the right call.

I had studied our route carefully, time and time again, and every photo and description indicated that the Headwall had deep boot holes for proper footholds as you ascended the line. However, this was the 2014 climbing season (*Outside* Magazine would title their Denali 2014 feature as "The Year of Mt. McKinley Summit Failure"), and the slick blue ice had glazed the entire face, so the points of our crampons could find little purchase. Without boot steps, all our weight was supported by the toe points of our crampons straining our calf muscles continuously to maintain a hold. Thankfully, a fixed rope was in place to arrest a fall. These were the only things keeping us fixed to the mountain.

As the Minnesotans descended, Team Salt Lake and Team Seattle progressed in the opposite direction. Brandon, Tom, and I moved like a synchronized crew, "rowing" up the first section in fine fashion. We quickly caught up to the tail end of a guided group. As "Pete" should have recognized and ultimately discovered, on a big mountain, with its legions of roped teams, going around is not an option—or certainly not one that is recommended if you desire to return home safe.

Unfortunately, our rowing style that had served us so well was slowed to a doggy paddle as the slowest common denominator in the group ahead set everyone's speed.

Eventually, the guided groups decided to take a break and move off the route, and we jumped at our chance. Passing 30 climbers (five six-man rope teams) in mere minutes, we quickly progressed up the route. Our training and experience allowed us the opportunity to avoid a summit-killing bottleneck. Realizing that this was the final section and we had to make a decisive move, we asked the lead professional guide of the guided group in front of us if we could hop on the fixed rope of the Headwall. He asked, in a condescending tone, if we had an ascender (a safety device secured to your harness that freely slides up but bites the rope if there's any downward pressure). We did, and quickly moved up the line, although with trepidation. Despite the harness, which is connected to the ascender and "grips" you to the rope, it is intimidating to rely on such a small and simple handheld device. Truthfully, the way up is with your feet, more specifically, the ¼ inch steel points of your crampons that sink into the ice and bear your entire body weight. Over and over, we would anchor to the headwall with our ice axes, unclip from the safety line to move past an anchor point, then connect it to the other side of the fixed anchor and then unclip our ascender and repeat. We did this process for an hour and a half without pause until we reached the top of the Headwall. By this time, even though we started only a few minutes apart, Team Seattle was at least an hour behind us, unable to advance in the queue of the other guided groups, all slowly advancing on the fixed lines.

An ascent of Denali rarely gives respite, and too soon our next challenge was in front of us. The ridge that leads from the Headwall to High Camp is somewhat precarious. As mentioned, roped teams must feed their line though fixed ropes held with ice anchors; in the event of a fall, a climber would only fall the distance of the current section—their fall arrested where the anchor was placed. When we climbed up this section, the winds from the north side of the mountain (from which we had been previously protected) struck us with full force. There are no timeouts when you are in this position on a mountain, you simply have to push through or retreat. There is usually no shelter on a ridge. And wind, more than any other factor, has a menacing way of relentlessly stripping body heat in concert with your will to continue. About this time, I observed that Tom, who was on the rope below me, was completely gassed. His head hung as if being snapped by a hangman. He did his best to stay upright and continued climbing, but he was obviously becoming hypothermic. I knew exactly how he felt. On our climb to Mt. Elbrus in Russia just 11 months earlier, we had been climbing through the night for our summit attempt in similar winds and temperatures, and I began to uncontrollably shake, and my teeth began to chatter. Tom was right next to me, helping me take a minute and offering encouraging words: "You got this, drink hot tea and put on your down coat." It worked like a charm.

Fortunately, we were positioned by the only section on the ridge that offered any sort of protection, a 20-foot high outcropping of rock called Washburn's Thumb. This provided the wind barricade we desperately needed. Remembering how the hot drink brought me back on Elbrus, I tugged on the rope separating me from Brandon and motioned him back down the ridge—he had already been pushed ahead, past the rock and climbing continuously upward. The three of us huddled behind Washburn's Thumb as I pulled our white gas stove from my pack and feverishly lit it, pouring my ice-cold grape Gatorade into the pot. What takes a few seconds to boil at sea level takes an eternity at high altitude, and it must have been fifteen minutes before we could heat it sufficiently. We did our best to keep the wind from extinguishing our flame, as well as keeping ourselves from getting senseless from the cold. Once the brew was hot enough, Tom drank it greedily. The instant effect the drink had on him was simply dramatic. It was as if he was a video game character down to the last percent of life who comes upon a Full Life pellet.

With Tom revived, we continued our climb, but the weather was turning from bad to worse, and we began to see every group far behind us, one by one, do an about-face and head back down the mountain, effectively abandoning their shot at the top. One group, I noticed, was walking in circles, stuck in an endless loop like patients in a mental ward. I knew they were desperately moving to stay warm, trying to decide if they could continue upward into the abyss or retreat like all the others. With every group turning around, I looked up to Brandon, and for the first and only time, I was truly terrified in the mountains. I yelled across the void, my voice barely discernable amidst the howling wind, "Brandon, what do we do?" Without hesitation and with the confidence of a doubtless leader, he said simply, "We keep going." And with that, he turned upward into the gale and began to lead us again to High Camp. Endlessly, Brandon placed protection into the mountain and safely followed the fixed ropes as we firmly placed each step until we rolled over a pass. Thinking that this was our final push before safety, we reached the plateau, only to see in the swirling snowstorm, more mountain and, far off in the distance, a few barely discernable orange dots. Those dots, we all knew, were the tents at our final camp, seemingly miles away...

Two hours later, we finally shuffled into High Camp, moving like the walking dead. Exhausted, the wind blowing mercilessly, we knew we still had to saw out blocks of snow for a wind wall and set up our 3-man tent. While lower camps are organized with paths and relatively sculpted tent platforms, the final camp on Denali is one of "drop gear and set up where you can." With barely the energy to stand, we used a partial wall of a Korean group, added some discarded blocks for a bit of a wind shelter and unraveled our tent—on which I immediately lay to prevent our only hope of respite from flying off the 17,000-foot North Face, one of the greatest unobstructed vertical drops in the world. Tom and Brandon buried our snow stakes at the corners of the tent and used our ice axes and trekking poles for every tent loop and guy line. Once set up, we all collapsed through the door at the same time and just lay there. No words were spoken; none were needed. The only sound was the thrashing of tent fabric against each other. With the firm conviction of Brandon's mountain mindset to safely continue, he had stretched us to the limit and in so doing, put us in a position to summit.

Just as my eyelids were mercifully closing for what I hoped would be a long sleep, they snapped open as our radio crackled. "Dave, this is Luke (Team Seattle), do you copy?" Had they not turned around? Luke indicated that they were above the Headwall and were wondering about continuing. I told them this was the most exhausting stretch any of us had experienced on any mountain. I think they recognized the defeat in my voice, and after a moment Luke came back with, "Okay we're going to set up and sleep on the ridge." They, too, realized that if they headed back down the Headwall, they might not make it back up. There was one other group who toughed it out, the group circling like zombies; that group was guided by Brent Okita, whom I'll talk about in Chapter 4.

On that mountain ridge, Tom had nearly passed out, and I was more terrified than I had ever been—and, as it turns out, would ever be. But Brandon had not hesitated, and his determined mindset of "we keep going" positioned us to take advantage of one of the only summit days available that year. In 2014, there was no second chance. My friend Dan, whom I'd later climb Everest with, was in one of the many commercially guided groups that turned back, and in so doing missed his summit opportunity on Denali.

It takes an enormous amount of physical training, courage, and risk tolerance to be a successful mountain climber.

But even if you are the most physically trained and courageous person on earth and a genius at assessing and balancing risk and rewards, you will still fail if you don't have what I call a *mountain mindset*. The mountain mindset consists of three core elements: Absolute Belief, Total Preparation, and Unwavering Ascent.

The phrase, the mountain mindset, is carefully chosen. How many mountain climbers do you know? How many people do you know who have endured the hardships, pain, and fear required to reach the summit of a mountain and been able to enjoy that exhilarating feeling on a mountaintop that's unlike any other? Very few? You don't climb a mountain—you don't put your life at risk—if you believe you will never reach the summit. You don't put your life at risk on a mountain if you don't take every step to prepare in every way possible and in anticipation of any hurdle or setback that might lay ahead. You don't reach the mountaintop unless you refuse to turn around when the easier, less painful path is to descend.

In many ways, climbing a mountain is a unique experience. *But in many ways, it is not.*

Whether it's the rich-and-famous superstar athlete or musician; the powerful CEO who has the ultimate responsibility for the success of a billion-dollar company; the professional whose life is filled with a successful career, a happy family, a beautiful home, the perks of affluence including traveling and a beach house—all of these people and more have climbed their mountain, because reaching their summit was no easier than reaching the mountain summits that you'll read about in this book. The dangers were not the same, the preparation was not the same, the work was not the same; but their mindset was the same. They all ultimately believed that they could succeed, even if there were moments of doubt—and you know by now that those moments occur on any mountain. They all took the time and care to prepare for success. And they refused to turn around.

How many mountain climbers do you know? A whole lot more than you think.

In this book, we will focus on the elements of the mountain mindset that all successful people share: the importance of believing in yourself, of fully preparing for the effort, and of not accepting easy defeat.

From academic research and from the lives of ordinary people who have accomplished the impossible, you'll find that persistence is a choice. Those who fail to reach life's summits do so not because of external circumstances, but because they make the conscious decision not to persist. No matter what their talents and attributes, they are unable to cross the inevitable deep crevasses that they encounter in the pursuit of any goal because they believe that there are limits to what they can accomplish. They take setbacks and failures as signals that it's time to give up.

If you are starting to lose touch with your mountain mindset, you can turn it around. By focusing on the summit and refusing to be consumed by the valleys, you'll find that you can persist, that you can overcome the challenges, that you can succeed. There's an old, boring saying: it's all in your mind. You might believe that it's a bit naïve or simplistic to insist that "it's all in your mind." Well, as a group of Ivy-league researchers proved, that old saying is right on the money.

CAROL DWECK'S TWO MINDSETS

We were now entering our third week of climbing Denali. Today was the day we had been working towards. All of the time, energy, and effort came to this: we were finally setting out for the summit. The winds had abated, the cloud cover that had enveloped us had mercifully cleared, and the sky was a smooth shade of purple—it looks that way when you're 17,000 feet up in thin, clean air. It was a stark contrast from our previous days as we stumbled to High Camp only able to see a few feet in front of us.

As we were making our final preparations before leaving our tent, I observed a group of four climbers who were ascending the Autobahn, a steep slope outside our camp that must be climbed before reaching the other section of the mountain. It's crudely named after a German group of climbers who slid to their deaths on this section. According to the National Park Service, this section has been the scene of more fatalities on Denali than any other part of the mountain. The group of four climbers had stopped halfway on the slope and were obviously deliberating about something for quite some time. I then noticed one climber turn and head back towards our High Camp. *Was something wrong with the route?* He was way too far into the climb to quit, especially when the weather was ideal. We were ready to set out and begin when this climber finally reached camp. With his long hair, gaunt features, and scruffy beard, he could easily pass for a member of the Bee Gees, but several weeks on a high mountain will do that to you. As he passed, I had so many questions, but I simply asked, "Hey, how's it going up there?" His response caught me off guard: "It's just not for me."

What!? Everyone who's made it to this point has been climbing for weeks, in the worst weather in four decades, and when we finally have one day of bluebird skies, it's just not for you? I don't know what happened to this Brother Gibb, but his defeated declaration is what led me to writing this book.

Why are some people able to persist in the face of setbacks while others fold? Why do some people rise to challenges while others do everything to avoid them? And why, under the exact same conditions, circumstances, and ability, do some people reach life's summits, while others turn back?

I think a possible answer comes from Stanford psychology professor Carol Dweck's research on the personal motivations and thought processes that enable some to succeed while others fail. This research led to her discovery of two mindsets: a *fixed* mindset, and a *growth* mindset.

The fixed mindset is the belief that a person is born with a fixed set of talents and skills, and any success has to be built on those innate attributes. The growth mindset is the belief that any person can grow their talents and skills.

In her best-selling book, *Mindset: The New Psychology of Success*, Dweck explains why the fixed mindset is damaging to success. First, having a fixed mindset causes people to stay within the narrow limits of what they consider to be the reach of their attributes. They will be afraid to try something that may be too difficult because they don't want to show others the "boundaries" of their talents and skills—what they are not smart enough or talented enough to achieve. In short, people with a fixed mindset are afraid of challenges that might unmask deficiencies that they think they can never improve on or resolve. A poor public speaker with a fixed mindset would never join Toastmasters, because he or she believes that some people are great in front of an audience and other people are failures who will be painful (or at least boring) to watch—and nothing can change that fact.

People with a growth mindset have a completely different attitude about challenges. If people with a fixed mindset believe that challenges and obstacles will shine a spotlight on what they'll never be able to accomplish or achieve, people with a growth mindset have the opposite view. They welcome challenges and obstacles because they offer a chance to advance, to increase capacity, to achieve something that they've never achieved before. I have climbed the world's highest peaks, but I didn't start off assuming that I had all the innate talent to become a skilled mountaineer. Instead, I had the *growth mindset* that I could learn to climb the highest mountains in the world, and this mindset helped me persist in acquiring the skills and experiences needed to give me a chance high on a mountaintop.

Of course, not all people are the same. There are innate talents and skills—some people will naturally hit high notes or pull down more rebounds, or some people will retain and recall information leading to better test-taking than others. I am certainly not physically gifted: I've never been the strongest climber on any of our expeditions. The point of Dweck's research is not that everybody can achieve everything—that if you want to be a professional basketball player all you have to do is to have the right mindset. The point is that *all of us* can grow our skills and talents. Even the greatest superstars in their fields succeeded not because they had the greatest talent, but because they built on their innate talents: through hard work and intense focus, they took what they had and developed it.

In her book, Dweck describes how she asks the students of her freshman class to research and write a short biography of their heroes. Many of these students assume that their heroes catapulted to great heights in their fields because of their talents. They discover, however, that in almost every case, these high achievers overcame setbacks and challenges and grew whatever innate skills and talents through very hard work. Even Michael Jordan did not have superior innate basketball skills—he acquired them through hundreds of hours of practice, going back to middle school.

HOW MINDSET CHANGES EVERYTHING— EVEN YOUR BRAIN

For some people, stress is a motivator and an energizer. They are more productive and more effective under stress. For others, stress drains their energy and increases their anxiety, making them less productive and effective. A series of studies by Yale University, using a new test called the Stress Mindset Measure (SMM), showed that neither the amount of stress nor one's ability to cope with stress was the deciding factor on whether the study's participants found stress to be energizing or debilitating. The deciding variable: your perspective on stress. Stress is debilitating to most people because most people think that stress is debilitating!

Having shown that mindset is the deciding factor on whether stress is going to increase or reduce your effectiveness, the Yale researchers wondered whether mindset could be changed. To find out, they asked participants—the same 400 employees of a large financial institution who had participated in the first study—to watch one of two series of videos: one series emphasized the *benefits* of stress, one emphasized the *harm* of stress. A few days later, they took the SMM test again. They also took tests measuring work performance and the psychological state of the participants. The results: watching a stress-is-debilitating video was enough to instill a stress-is-debilitating mindset—and again, once they had that mindset, participants suffered from the psychological symptoms and poor performance of people negatively impacted by stress. The stress-is-positive video, you won't be surprised to hear, had the opposite effect.

How can mindset have such an effect on what you probably believed was just your natural and logical response to stress? It turns out that there's some biology involved, and it involves the fluctuation of a chemical called cortisol in your brain. Your level of cortisol decides how you respond to a stimulant—whether you are going to be calm or excited. Of course, not everybody has the same cortisol levels—some people get excited easily, others are unflappable. I have come to understand with my own physiology and cortisol levels that when I feel a level of angst many mornings, it's simply due to the adrenal glands and the cortisol awakening response (CAR). I also know that simply getting out of bed, standing up, and moving forward greatly diminishes this angst and corrects me back to normal. What the Yale researchers found was that the right mindset about stress—in other words, the mindset that stress is a positive thing that helps rather than hurts your effectiveness—actually takes your cortisol up or down to its optimal level (the optimal level being that you neither overreact nor under-react to stimuli). In other words, according to this study, your mindset can *change the chemicals in your brain* to make you deal better with stress. That's the power of mindset.

CONQUERING DISABILITIES: WHAT THE MOUNTAIN MINDSET CAN ACHIEVE

No matter what you attempt, no matter what your goal or ambition might be, there will come a time when you face serious and often unexpected setbacks, challenges, and failures. It is not a question of "if" but of "when." On our Everest summit attempt, I remember climbing higher and higher into the Death Zone, the memory of the frozen corpse still replaying in my mind. With each step the wind was gaining strength and getting stronger. The winds had been 40-50 mph, knocking me a little off balance, when a 90-mph gust blasted our team and would have knocked us off the mountain had we not been connected to the rope. When these gusts come in your life, you have two choices: get swept off the mountain or *lean in*. Lean into the challenge, lean into the trial. As I look back on my personal life, these unexpected gusts come every nine months or so. You get hit with a child taking a different direction, a job loss or unexpected financial stressor, cancer or illness. If you can understand that gusts will come, you can prepare to lean in, dig in, and keep climbing.

The question is, how will you react? What separates those who succeed from those who fail is not the strength of the gusts or number of mountains they had to face but whether or not their mindset prepared them to deal with those challenges. With the mountain mindset, you can persist in the face of a seemingly insurmountable climb. If you don't believe me, if you think your challenges are way too big to be conquered by mindset, here are some people I want you to meet.

DON'T LET DETOURS STOP THE JOURNEY

For most young basketball players, playing in the NBA is their ultimate dream, but for as long as he can remember, Karl Turk had just one goal in life: to be a basketball coach. At 5 years old, he stood up and announced to his family at the dining room table: "I'm going to be a basketball coach." As he was playing basketball for his middle school team in Indiana, the dream continued: I'm going to be a basketball coach. And then one morning, at the age of 14, Karl woke up paralyzed from the waist down, caused by an infection that had suffocated his spine. The doctors told his parents that he would not live through the following night. But after 65 nights in intensive care, Karl Turk was still alive. The doctors insisted, however, that he would never walk again. As he left the hospital in a wheelchair, it would seem that the dream had died. His basketball playing days were over. And so were his chances of ever becoming a basketball coach…

Karl Turk, however, persisted in his dream. Since he could not play basketball—his legs were still encased in braces—he worked as the manager of his team in high school. At Indiana State, the alma mater of Larry Bird, he harangued Sycamores coach Royce Waltman until Waltman let him become team manager. Eventually, he was able to walk again, although painfully, slowly, and with a cane. After college, he applied for jobs as a camp counselor at basketball camps. He knew that if he wanted to be a coach some day, he had to work as many camps as possible. When applying, he never bothered to mention that he was disabled; the organizers of the camps would find out when he showed up. By then it was too late to get another counselor, and so Turk kept the job. He still has on an index card the list of all the camps from 2004 that he targeted for jobs.

There were lean times, several years where he had no job and could not even get an interview. On another index card, Turk also has the list of the schools and coaches who refused to see him. Those were his motivation to continue.

Eventually, after all the basketball camps, and finally acquiring some experience as an assistant, the dream came true: he was offered a job as a basketball coach at West Oso High School in Corpus Christi, Texas. Turk, however, did not just want to be a basketball coach, he wanted to be a *successful* basketball coach, and that dream is also a reality. Under his leadership, West Oso High School is a perennial state champion, an impressive record for a state as large and populated as Texas.

Karl Turk achieved his dream for one reason and one reason only: his mindset. Without the mental toughness to fight for his dream in the face of insurmountable odds (starting with a life-changing physical disaster that came from nowhere), without his persistence in the face of so many refusals, Turk would have never coached a single game.

How does he do it? By refusing to accept himself as disabled. Turk is not just someone who doesn't dwell on his disability; he is someone whose disability is so far out of his mind that he sometimes falls down because he *forgets* he can't walk! The boys he coaches have seen it happen numerous times, and as one player told a local newspaper, you better keep focused on the game, and not on the fact that your coach has fallen on his backside, because the coach is still coaching, and if he sees you let up…

Turk's mindset is exceptional, and perhaps he had a little help building it. All those years ago, when he was still in the hospital, the door to his room opened and in walked Indiana Pacers legend Reggie Miller. "Aren't you… you?" stammered Turk. It was indeed *him*. Miller explained to Turk that he himself had been in braces for years as a child. And yet he had persisted.

ATTEMPT THE IMPOSSIBLE

Lee Ridley, a native of Newcastle, England, thought being a stand-up comedian would be the greatest job in the world. Ridley, however, believed it was not a possible career for him for a very simple and understandable reason: how can you be a stand-up comedian when you are unable to speak? After a brain infection when he was just a toddler put him in a coma for two weeks, Lee Ridley developed cerebral palsy and, in his life, has never been able to utter a single word. He does communicate through an iPad, which generates a computerized voice, and in the opinion of his friends, that was good enough. They pushed him and pushed him until finally he decided he would try to become the world's first stand-up comedian with cerebral palsy—because he knew he would regret it if he never gave it a try.

The success of his first gig gave Ridley, taking the stage name Lost Voice Guy, courage to try for a comedy career. Lost Voice Guy skyrocketed to international fame as a comedian after winning the TV talent show, *Britain's Got Talent.* More than 15 million viewers around the world have watched his comedy on YouTube.

Like Karl Turk, Ridley refuses to be defined by his disability. Ridley and Turk have the opposite of what experts call "the disability mindset." The disability mindset occurs when someone becomes ill or is injured and is temporarily unable to work. Instead of recovering or overcoming the barriers erected by the injury, people with the disability mindset become fixated on the disability and can only think about what they *cannot* do, instead of what they can do.

Turk and Ridley have a different view of their disabilities completely. For Turk, the disability is not disabling—he in essence ignores his disability (and in fact, forgets it so much that he falls down). Ridley uses his disability to inspire his comedy: "As you've gathered by now, I'm a stand-up comedian who can barely stand up."

HOW TO LEVERAGE MINDSET

The stories above involve two courageous people who overcame their disabilities. Hearing such stories, of course, can be somewhat daunting: "I would never have done what they did if I were in their shoes," you might think. Here are two important lessons that show you *how* to leverage a positive mountain mindset—even if you don't think you're that extraordinary.

BE YOURSELF AND TAKE SMALL STEPS

Joy Mangano's story sounds extraordinary: a single mom, tired of getting her hands soaked by dirty water, invents a new mop to do something about it. It is story of amazing persistence. She spent years developing prototypes of the self-wringing mop until she found the perfect design, searching for and finally finding a manufacturer, and trying to sell her mop through stores and being constantly refused. For a while, she would sell her mop in parking lots.

Mangano thought that she had a made a major breakthrough when the television shopping network QVC agreed to sell her mops on the air. Not so fast. Sales were slow, and QVC notified her that they would be sending back the unsold inventory and ending the relationship. Desperate, Mangano asked QVC to let her go on the air and sell the mop herself. Skeptical, QVC executives gave her one shot. As she went before the cameras on that day in 1992, Mangano knew that the future of her business career was at stake. Speaking without a script, Mangano talked to viewers as if they were in her living room. In 20 minutes, she had sold 18,000 mops and had taken the first step toward her extraordinary success.

Here's the lesson about this story of persistence. You remember my friend Larry and his dream to enter the Iditarod race. He moved his family to Alaska to make his dream come true, which is incredible. But you don't necessarily have to make such a huge commitment to persist at something. Mangano didn't uproot her life, she didn't mortgage her house, she didn't sacrifice everything to make it big. Instead, she continued to be a conscientious and loving mother to her children and continued to go to work at her day job, while working on the prototype of her mop at night.

It's true that there are many stories of entrepreneurs who maxed out their credit cards, and I know too well about mortgaging the house for a business idea. And one might believe that being unwilling to "bet the farm" is an insurmountable barrier to becoming an entrepreneur.

For Mangano, this assumption that entrepreneurial success depends on a fearless mindset is one of the biggest myths of entrepreneurs. According to her, you don't have to "jump off a cliff," you don't have to do something crazy to get started. Just believe in yourself and take the first small step.

KNOW THE DIFFERENCE BETWEEN OPTIMISM AND DELUSION

While the mindset of persistence is one of optimism and a belief that the impossible is achievable, it is not the mindset of recklessness and foolishness. The persistent mindset is one of believing in the achievement of the impossible, but this belief is built on some foundation.

Carol Dweck does not argue in her book that anyone can become Michael Jordan with hard work; she only argues that *Michael Jordan* became Michael Jordan because of hard work. His mindset leveraged the innate talents he possessed into world-class abilities. When he attempted to break the four-minute mile, Roger Bannister had not wandered onto the track from the street; he was an experienced runner and a scientist who had studied the physics behind running. Joy Mangano was a born inventor: as a teenager, she had invented a flea collar for pets that was visible at night just months before the leading manufacturer of flea collars came out with an identical product. Mangano swore at that time that the next time she had an idea she believed in, she would do everything to bring it to market.

Finally, Lee Ridley overcame incredible disabilities to become a comedian. Ridley, however, *is a funny person.* The one insurmountable obstacle to be a successful comedian is not being funny. And if you're not funny, no amount of optimism or persistence is going to change that.

Every one of these achievers had some foundation of talent, skills, or personality on which to build. The world, however, is filled with talented, smart people who never achieve success. And probably, in nearly every case, the reason they were not able to leverage their attributes was because they didn't have the mountain mindset.

HOW TO CHANGE YOUR MINDSET

How, then, can you gain the mountain mindset and be more persistent in the future? I go back to Carol Dweck for the answer, which is that you can change your mindset when you become aware that there are two opposing voices in your head, and *it's your choice* which voice you want to listen to.

Listen to the Right Voices in Your Head

According to Dweck, people are overcome by challenges, setbacks, or even criticism because they *listen to the fixed mindset voices in their heads.* In the face of challenges, she writes, these voices will say such things as, "You're going to fail and everybody will see you fail." Like in Rocky, we all have our Adrian squawking at us from a long alley or the top of a dark staircase, and the words are always the same: "You can't win!" When setbacks occur, the voices will say, "I told you so, now you have failed and everyone knows it," or "If you really had talent, you would have succeeded." And when someone faces criticism, their fixed mindset voices will say, "It's not your fault, it's the others' fault," or "How dare they treat me like this?"—even if the criticism is constructive and fair.

The first step in replacing a fixed mindset with a growth mindset is to recognize that the voices exist, *and they are trying to influence you.* Those voices echo in your head, replaying continually. Some echoes are soft, vibrating in the distance, while others are loud and at the forefront. Those echoes, so clearly expressed in the previous paragraph, actually enter your consciousness in much more subtle ways. So, step one of acquiring the right mindset is, "**Learn to hear your fixed mindset voice and what echoes it will create.**"

The second step: **recognize that you have a choice.** Nothing is decided in advance; how you react to challenges or setbacks is *your decision.* You can decide to embrace the fixed mindset and interpret challenges and setbacks as proof of your deficiencies. Or, you can embrace the growth mindset as a signal to, in Dweck's words, "ramp up your strategies and effort, stretch yourself, and expand your abilities."

Step three: **talk back to your fixed mindset voice with your growth mindset voice**. In the face of a challenge, the fixed mindset voice will say, "Why bother, I don't have the talent." Answer with your growth mindset voice, echoing, "Maybe I can't do it now, but with time and effort, I can learn to do it." We know that in 1953, Edmund Hillary was immortalized by summiting Everest. What you may not know is that in 1952, he failed in his first attempt. Several weeks after coming home, he was asked to address a group of alpine climbers in England. Hillary walked on stage to thunderous applause. They were validating his attempt at greatness. But Hillary saw himself as a failure. Concluding his presentation, he stepped back from the microphone and walked to the edge of the platform. He made a fist then pointed at a picture of Mt. Everest.

He said in a loud voice, "Mount Everest, you beat me the first time, but I'll beat you the next time because you've grown all you are going to grow...but I'm still growing!"

The same battle will occur when facing a setback. The fixed mindset will view it as a step back while the growth mindset will view it as a step up. The fixed mindset voice will say, "If you had talent, this setback would not have occurred." Conjure up your growth mindset voice to answer, "Michael Jordan was bad at basketball, and Thomas Edison was poor at science, and yet they reached the pinnacles of their professions."

Finally, when in the face of criticism, the fixed mindset voice says, "This is not my fault," let your growth mindset voice respond, "Let me listen to the criticism and learn from it." Compliments comfort, but criticism corrects. Know the value between which comments will help and which need to be ignored. As it's been said, there's never been a statue built for a critic.

Now that you've given the fixed mindset voice in your head his say, the final step is to **take the growth mindset action**. You've listened to both voices. Decide to take the growth mindset action as opposed to the fixed mindset action. This means, Dweck writes, taking on challenges wholeheartedly, learning from setbacks and trying again, and heeding the criticism.

Often, the fixed mindset path will seem the most tempting. But the more you take the growth mindset action, and the more you see it work for you, the easier it will become to persist in the future, no matter what challenges and setbacks may try to stop you.

TURN OFF THE MUSIC, TURN ON THE MIND

I live the growth mindset every day by taking every opportunity I can to learn. The biggest single gains I made toward success and achievement is when I decided to turn off the music and turn on the mind. When I had a morning commute, I thought of what Brian Tracy said years ago: the average American commuter drives 12,000-15,000 miles a year, spending 500 to 1,000 hours behind the wheel. This is the same as two full university semesters each year.

So, you can turn your car into an audio university. Nothing has furthered my personal progression faster and farther than informational audio books. They have been the single biggest enhancement for my personal and professional progress in life.

And they are not just for the car. Whether I'm at the gym, on a flight, mowing the lawn, vacuuming—any time that I used to listen to my favorite playlist, I now use those countless hours to listen to the most recent books or podcasts on success, strategy, sales, or any number of topics that move me to where I want to be.

As Brian Tracy explained, "No one lives long enough to learn everything they need to learn starting from scratch. To be successful, we absolutely, positively have to find people who have already paid the price to learn the things that we need to learn to achieve our goals." There's a lifetime of knowledge that an author has poured into a best-selling book. It's been rewritten, edited, scoured, and endured years of drafts and research. And it's all there in a few hundred pages or a few hours of listening during your mind-free time.

This discipline of pouring the right sound into my ears has far outweighed or given me more to further my education than any time I spent in my undergraduate or graduate work, period. Believe me, you will see the biggest gains you can by turning off the music or the talk radio and investing instead in a monthly audio book account. This effort will pay consistent dividends larger than any other medium.

I also take, on average, one day a week where I commute in silence. I often receive so much great content that I need to just decompress with nothing! And a funny thing happens in silence. You can listen to what you really need to hear.

THE UNWRITTEN RULE: IT DOESN'T HAVE TO BE FUN TO BE FUN

I close this chapter with one of the lessons on mindset that I've drawn from my mountaineering experiences: the power of fulfillment. If you are enjoying the journey, your echoes are building the mountain mindset that will keep you persisting in the face of even the greatest challenges. If, on the other hand, you are not taking any pleasure in your climb, the negative voices will take over your mind at every obstacle, screaming to retreat, to go down, to quit.

I was in my mid-twenties, sitting at my cubicle, working for a telecom company in Salt Lake City when my friend and coworker Lance sits down on my desk and says, "I'm going to climb Mt. Rainier, and you're going to climb it with me."

Uh, what? I had no idea what he was talking about...? "What's Mt. Rainier?" I asked. Lance proceeds to commandeer my computer, pulls up an image of a snow-capped mountain, and begins to describe how he discovered in his research that it's the most heavily glaciated peak in the lower 48 states, making it one of the most challenging mountaineering climbs in the US: more people have died on Rainier than Everest, he says. How's that for a sales pitch! Lance was relentless, and his enthusiasm was contagious. However, it took several weeks of nonstop pestering until, and I'm still not sure when or why, I said okay. I'd never been to the top of anything. I'd never set a goal to climb to the top of anything—as a matter of fact, I hated hiking growing up. I never made it past a Tenderfoot in Boy Scouts. It's interesting that at the moment in time when we make a decision that will forever affect the path of our life, we are rarely aware that we just made such a momentous decision. Simply by agreeing to go, and do something unique and uncomfortable, my life took on a whole new path.

I soon found myself training with Lance, and since we were going to guide ourselves to the top, we thought it would be a really good idea to take a winter mountaineering course. We had since roped my boss, Chad, into climbing Mt. Rainier with us, so the three of us took the course and prepared for our early July attempt.

July 7, 2004, the day of our departure, arrived and for the first time in my life, I was going to attempt to scale a mountain peak. Mt. Rainier, located in the Cascade Range of the Pacific Northwest, is one of a series of peaks in arguably one of the most beautiful mountain ranges in the world. Its peaks are characterized by sweeping vistas, deep snowfields, and moderately steep glaciers that are bisected with crevasses. On clear days, you can see the not-so-distant peaks: Baker, Adams, Hood, and St. Helens. As with most higher-altitude peaks, the weather can be fickle and is dependent on the time of year of your summit bid and traditional weather patterns—you play the odds and hope the weather cooperates.

We woke up at 6:00 a.m. that morning, still uncertain if we would be climbing in snow flurries or not. Gray skies and low-hanging clouds had moved in and portended we'd be battling some weather. At any rate, I ate a quick breakfast of granola cereal at the

Paradise Inn. My bronchitis was in full swing, and if I exhaled fully, the audible cracking in my lungs could be heard by anyone nearby. After checking in with the park ranger and picking up our sanitary waste bags —called "blue bags" among other more desultory names—we were off.

The trailhead starts in the main parking lot of the Mt. Rainier National Park visitor's center with the first mile or so and 1,000 vertical feet traveled on a paved trail. After that, you reach the lower slope of the massive Muir snowfield, and the more difficult climbing begins. Once on the snow, our feet wouldn't touch anything different until we were inside the public shelter at Camp Muir.

For the next three-plus miles we headed straight up the Muir snowfield, gaining another 3,000 vertical feet. Our view was limited to 20 feet in any direction due to the clouds bogging us in. Step after annoying step, we walked into what seemed oblivion. It's an isolating experience when climbing in poor weather. Instead of majestic views and wide expanses, your world shrinks to a small sphere immediately surrounding you. While we were climbing during the day at this time, this is especially true when climbing at night in wind and snow flurries. It's easy to be lulled into a semi-aware state when your senses are deprived and communication is stilted—not to mention the physical process of climbing. This was my first real experience with that sensation.

After six hours of climbing, we finally heard a collection of voices through the clouds giving us an indication that we were closing in on Camp Muir. At last we had arrived. We located the public shelter (a narrow structure with two rows of plywood bunks and tables for gear and cooking) and found that no one else was there yet. We decided to stay in the shelter rather than setting up our own tent and having to tear it down the next morning. A few others soon joined us, which made for an eventful evening inside a soon-to-be-crowded shelter. Winds rattled the loose tin roof for most of the night. Earplugs were essential for enjoying any semblance of sleep. Few are able to sleep well in shelters like this, with every rustle of fabric, cough, and creak of the door drawing you back to consciousness. "Interesting" smells are also a constant presence.

The next morning, after reloading our packs, we made our way across the long traverse of the Cowlitz Glacier to the base of Cathedral Gap, which is essentially a rock scramble of tenuous footing in the scree (a steep mass of rock fragments that can accumulate at the base of mountains and cliffs from years of rockfalls). We headed up and over, gaining another 1,200 vertical feet until we arrived at our final camp, Ingerham Flats.

We were first to arrive again, which gave us first dibs on the abandoned snow platforms of the previous day's climbers. The weather cleared, and a hot afternoon was spent setting up crevasse rescue systems and reviewing the basics we learned in our mountaineering course several months before. We rested a bit, melted snow for our water reserves for the next day, and made dinner. We turned in at 6:00 p.m., but I found it impossible to sleep. As the hours passed by—7:00 p.m., 8:00 p.m., 9:00 p.m.— all I could do was think about the unknown. While there are over a dozen different ways to reach the summit, we had selected the Disappointment Cleaver route. It's aptly named. According to the

National Park Service, less than half (44 percent) of self-guided groups reach the summit. Going with a guide increases that to 60 percent, but also increases the cost from a $50 climbing permit if you're self-guided to $1600 to climb with a guide. We had ambition, not cash. 10:00 p.m. passed then 11:00 p.m., and still I tossed and turned and didn't sleep a single minute. I tried to take my mind off the task before us, but I kept coming back to the route, the challenge, the preparation, which all combined for the sleepless night. Finally, 12:00 a.m. came and we were up and making our preparations. At 1:00 am, an Alpine start, we were on the trail. I remember staring down upon the clouds, the majestic sky lit by a half moon. It's a memory that will always stay with me. A memory that has led me back to climb Mt Rainier nearly every year since.

Chad's and my crampons popped off a few times, but once fixed, we were off and running—although not literally, of course: we were following our usual rest, step, rest, step pace. The route quickly led us to the base of Disappointment Cleaver proper, another more difficult rock scramble. 1,100 feet of exposed trail with twists, awkward steps on, over, and around boulders, all the while listening for the tell-tale sounds of a rockfall. It's difficult to establish a rhythm while in the Cleaver, and the scraping of our crampons on rock accompanied us upward. Following thin bamboo wands stuck in the snow as route markers, and old crampon divots, we navigated our way up and out of the Cleaver.

Once we cleared that obstacle, we were welcomed by 40-plus mph winds—a frequent occurrence on Rainier. With the wind chill bringing the temp below zero, we climbed on at a steady pace.

Resting even for a couple of minutes would bring on uncontrollable shivering. By the final rest section known as High Break, my fatigue, bronchitis, dehydration, and lack of sleep all combined for a debilitating moment of desperation. I could only go at a snail's pace, so I suggested that Chad and my other climbing partner, Lance, go before me so I could have someone to follow. Wind swept the face of the mountain, scraping flecks of ice that felt like sandpaper across my exposed face. After the switch of our climbing positions, it seemed only a matter of moments before there was no longer any mountain above us.

We made it! The first ones on the route and the first ones to the top! A half-year of planning and preparations had finally paid off. We were victorious. As we sat on the Crater Rim, Lance was in bad shape and needing a quick descent. He apologized for this seemingly miserable experience, but as I looked over the sea of clouds that led to Seattle and beyond, watching the rise of the sun, I thought that this was one of the greatest experiences someone could feel in the mountains.

And that's all it took. As it turns out, this was Lance's last summit, even though he had been the instigator of the climb, while it was the first of many for me—and it altered my life forever. The fulfillment of mountaineering is often realized after you're off the mountain, when you're reflecting on the experience. It doesn't have to be fun, to be fun. You're only on the summit for a few minutes. Life's climb—whatever that climb is for you—can take weeks or months or years. Someone once told me that their greatest attribute in climbing mountains was the ability to climb hour-after-hour, straight up the side of a mountain—tired, sore, nauseous—and still have the time of their life. If you aren't having fun, you're doing something wrong.

The persistent mindset requires courage, resilience, and a strong belief in oneself. What is unsaid throughout all of the stories in this chapter is that the extraordinary people involved are enjoying themselves! Lee Ridley enjoys telling jokes, Joy Mangano enjoys creating new products that make life better, Karl Turk's love for basketball didn't end when abilities to play the game did, and I love the struggle, challenges, and bonds formed in the mountains. That's the growth mindset that keeps me coming back. In the words of Edmond Hillary: Have you grown all you can grow? Keep growing.

CHAPTER THREE

CHOOSE YOUR ROPE TEAM

The key is to keep company only with people who uplift you, whose presence calls forth your best.

— Epictetus

If you want to go fast, go alone. If you want to go far, go together.

— African Proverb

You are the average of the five people you spend the most time with.

— Jim Rohm

I've made it a rule to only have friends I've previously climbed with allowed on my big mountain expeditions. The majority of climbers who want to pursue high mountains don't have this luxury as it's typically a lonely man's pursuit, one that doesn't enlist your usual group of friends. These lonely climbers have to join a group of perfect strangers as part of a professionally guided expedition and have to play to the lowest common denominator of the group for how effectively (or ineffectively) they can progress on the mountain. They put their lives in the hands of an experienced guide, but also some dude from Delaware they've never met.

On most major glaciated peaks, you're tied together on a rope team of three to six climbers. There are often large cracks in the ice called crevasses hidden by fragile snow bridges. If the snow bridge collapses and you fall into the crevasse, the members of the rope team need to be there to self-arrest (stop the fall) by kicking in their crampons and landing their weight on the point of their axe. For this reason, you have to *know* that you can trust your rope team with your life.

When I first met Lardog, he was Brandon's friend, and Brandon invited him to climb Mt. Rainier with us. On our summit attempt, I was in the lead, with Lardog in the middle followed by Brandon at the end. We were traveling along a gently sloping area just below the Disappointment Cleaver when I felt a tug on the rope. I quickly looked back and saw Lardog had broken through a snow bridge and was suspended only by his shoulders, dangling in a crevasse below. I fell on my axe, as did Brandon and Lardog, and we were able to pull his body weight over the lip of the crevasse to safety. Even though Larry was a novice at the time, I was impressed with his calm demeanor and his ability to quickly and effectively react and extricate himself from the hazard. From that time forward, he forever earned a spot on my rope anytime.

The only time I've made an exception to my rule was on Denali, the highest peak in North America. Lardog couldn't make the climb, but my usual team of Tom and Brandon were on my rope (Team Salt Lake). We also had Cecil, Luke—both of whom I've climbed with on other mountains—and Cecil's friend whom we'll call "Jarret." This was Team Seattle, as mentioned previously. Jarret had the resume of a successful, competent climber. He spent three years guiding on Mt. Rainier, with extensive rock and ice experience, as well as several other high peaks to his credit. Cecil asked if he could join, as Jarret had always wanted to climb Denali, and on paper, he fit the bill. Through our pre-expedition planning, Jarret was very detail-oriented to the point that he wanted to ensure we had recently reviewed every aspect of crevasse rescue, the varying techniques of pulley systems to extract a fallen climber, the proper clothing layers to combat the subarctic temperatures found climbing Denali, and so on. Some of Jarret's suggestions and comments appeared excessive, but I respected and appreciated the preparation going into a mountain that has claimed the lives of less-prepared climbers.

I met Jarret in Anchorage in the lobby of the Microtel hotel. He was a short, slender guy with a quick return on any comment. My first impression was that he seemed to be a good fit with our team of six. We boarded our Econoline white van from a local logistics company appropriately named "ADVENTURE," and we set off to Talkeetna, the self-proclaimed "quaint little drinking town with a climbing problem" from where we would take flight for the mountain.

We checked in and weighed our gear with the air taxi that would be transporting us from the Talkeetna airport at an elevation of 300 feet to the start of our climb on the Kahiltna glacier at 7,200 feet.

Before we took flight, each climber was required to check in at the Denali Ranger station. You must be approved to climb their mountain with the right provisions before you're permitted to endanger your life and the lives of those you may need to call upon in rescue. We were greeted by an old timer who seemed to revel in the anxiety of first-time Denali climbers about to attempt "the

Great One"—as Denali's name is translated in the native Athabascan language.

After observing the group before us exit the training room white-faced and in a daze, we entered at our appointed schedule for our briefing. Our Denali Ranger—Ranger Rick, who had been a ranger for over 20 years—made quick work of the serious nature of climbing Denali. Before he dimmed the lights and started into his dated PowerPoint, he seemed pleased to describe the speed and efficiency with which a wounded climber with a serious head injury was just rescued and evacuated from the mountain. He marveled that the incident "happened only six hours ago and now she was in serious but stable condition at the Anchorage Regional hospital as we speak." Thanks for the pep talk, coach!

After a PowerPoint filled with photos of frostbitten fingers, crevasses, and climbers on stretchers, he reviewed our climbing resumes, gear, and with a final wry "good luck," we were out of there.

I felt confident in my preparations leading up to the climb, but for the first time, my distending stomach was telling me otherwise.

Back at the Talkeetna airport, weather reports were coming in that there may be no other opportunities for flights due to weather. We were waiting on standby until news reached that there would be one final flight out, and our number was called. We tagged our bags and loaded into the single engine plane. Luke, who's a professional photographer, was sitting shotgun with his full complement of photography gear. With the glass obstructing his shots, he opened the window as the plane took off, quickly cooling the cabin. Our irritated bush pilot obliged for the first few times but then let Luke know the next time something opened, Luke would be the one leaving the plane. I supposed I shouldn't ask for my six ounces of soda and peanuts.

Arriving at the airstrip, which is just a level snowbank on the glacier, the pilot worked on overdrive to throw our gear out and load the recently defeated climbers who looked like death warmed over. In a blink, we watched the single prop Turbo Otter disappear into the oncoming storm, cutting any ties we had to civilization and the comfortable world.

After digging a snow pit and caching some clean clothes and food in a Styrofoam cooler at the airstrip basecamp to have supplies on hand upon our return two or three weeks later, we took advantage of the overcast midnight bright skies and started climbing. Luke and Cecil left on skis, and the rest of us strapped on our snowshoes. The route starts at a comfortable descent known as Heartbreak Hill, a section that punishes every exhausted climber on the return. Its 600 feet of vertical climbing when your body is already depleted certainly adds insult to injury for climbers who return without a summit.

As a self-guided group, we had the luxury of setting our pace, schedule, and time for our Denali climb. About half of the 1,000-plus Denali climbers per year will set out without a professional guide service. Because guided commercial groups are at the mercy of their weakest client, they are required to double carry their loads. Double carry is when you move up the mountain with half your loaded weight, dig a storage in the snow, then retreat down the mountain to retrieve the other half and move it up on a second rotation. We, on the other hand, knew our group's strength and skill level and could carry our loads in a single push, which proved to be a speedy strategy for us.

After four hours of roped-up travel, we arrived at Camp 1 at 9,800 feet. We occupied a vacant campsite perfect for our three tents. With snow walls already surrounding the requisite ¾ of our site, we could relax and begin boiling snow—the nonstop chore on Denali.

Being roped together, you need to keep about 40-60 feet of rope between you to arrest a fall from your partner. This distance results in an isolating activity, but it can also give you a welcome break from teammates you may want to no longer communicate with! It didn't take but two days before our group dynamic changed in terrible fashion.

Early afternoon, several hours into our day's climb, we had taken a break to grab a snack. It was overcast with temperatures in the single digits and little wind. This felt like a comfortable temperature, and we had worked up a fine perspiration, so Luke took his gloves off for some finer adjustments on his backpack and gear. Jarret noticed this and immediately took issue: "Luke, it's frostbite temps out here, put your gloves on."

Since we're all experienced and competent climbers, we didn't think much about it as we're big boys and can care for ourselves. Luke responded, "I'm good, man." Jarret didn't find this acceptable. "This is the Arctic Circle, your hands will freeze and frostbite, put on your fucking gloves!" And just like that, Jarrett went from 0-60 mph in 2 seconds flat.

With an even tone, Luke replied, "Dude, this isn't my first rodeo, I know my body and I'm okay." Having guided for many seasons on Mount Rainier, Jarret wasn't one who took objection to his "requests" lightly on the mountains. "This is bullshit, I'm off this rope." And with that, Jarret switched places with Tom, and now I had the pleasure of having this thermal reactor climbing behind me on my rope. It wasn't a big thing replacing someone on my rope, but Brandon and Tom were my rope guys, on every climb, and I prefer to keep it that way.

With tempers, or I guess just one temper, still on Level 10, we shuffled at 11,000 feet into Camp 3, again a pre-made snow platform recently vacated by others, and made for a quick set up for the night. Divided among our three tents were Tom and I, Luke and Cecil, and Brandon and Jarret.

The next morning, I awoke to Jarret barking in Luke and Cecil's tent with his attack mode in full force: "You had no respect for our pre-planning meetings and training climbs. I would have rather been with my wife at Applebee's, but Cecil and I made the time to review our crevasse techniques, something you felt the need to skip." The one-way lecture continued for a time, but all I could think of was Applebee's as his go-to date night restaurant.

The nylon of our tents can thwart 100 mph winds, but offer the same sound privacy as a Japanese paper partition, and after 20 minutes of listening to Jarret drone on berating Luke, I could take no more.

I got dressed (ensuring I had gloves on), forced my way into their 3-man tent and interjected with my opinion: "There was a time where I spent two years of my life living with guys that I had no choice to be with. While I got along with most, I promised myself that once I was done with this service mission, I would only choose to be with individuals who uplift and inspire, who make me better. Jarret, no one seems to have a problem with Luke, so as I see it, you have two choices. Mountaineering is hard enough, and we're carrying enough weight without *this* extra baggage. You can choose to put the past behind, or you can end and descend, but this team I've assembled won't include another word of useless dialog."

Jarret snapped back with, "You need to understand that I..."

"Jarret, I do understand. But we're going to continue the next few weeks as a team with or without you." I left the tent, and Jarret didn't seem to need to speak further to Luke or Cecil and exited behind me.

He took some time to reflect and pulled me aside to say that he'd like to continue but didn't feel comfortable with Luke's disposition. And so it was, we would continue as a six-man team.

At Camp 3, we packed our provisions for the only time we had to do a double carry to cache, and for the first time, we were climbing without pulling our 70-pound sleds. We began to ascend Motorcycle Hill, a mile-long stretch, gaining 800 feet vertically. After crossing a small break in the slope angle called Squirrel Point, the winds suddenly hit us as if a dam had broken and released a mass of swirling, frozen air flooding us without mercy. Continual adjustments of my goggles, hood, and face buff proved no use as the wind continued to find any little slit or opening to flash freeze my face. At around 50-60 mph, wind can knock you off balance, and that's exactly what we were beginning to experience. We were still short of our cache location, but we knew that continuing in this weather would prove disastrous. Against Jarret's wishes, who wanted to continue, we axed and chipped away, creating a hole large enough for several duffels of our group gear and marked it with our 3 foot long bamboo stick markers topped with pink LOL duct tape my daughters wrapped around my trekking poles. After deciding that our pioneer prairie burial for our 150 pounds of food, fuel, and non-essential gear would be good, we turned our wind-blasted faces the other direction and headed back to camp.

For the next week and a half, we methodically progressed up the mountain, Jarret continuing to launch his verbal jabs, or interjecting useless mountain facts or "pro climbing tips" that no one solicited. We had picked the worst weather year on Denali, but on June 4th we were finally in a position to head for the summit.

On summit day, my trusted friends Tom and Brandon were on my rope. Cecil, Luke and Jarret were again bickering about something—possibly the uncanny resemblance of that Bee Gee-looking guy, but we set out for the top hoping they would soon catch up. Four hours passed, and my team was making steady progress with no sight of the Seattle guys, so we decided to take a break. Suddenly, I noticed a solo climber making his way up the mountain, and I immediately thought, "Who's this idiot climbing alone?" As he got closer, I thought it might be Cecil, as the climber was wearing his exact coat. Once in earshot, we heard a "Hey, guys" and when he drew near, I could see it was Jarret. "Where's your team?" I asked. He replied, "After Denali pass, my Spidey senses kicked in, and I didn't feel comfortable continuing to climb with those guys, so I felt it was best to go on alone." Dumbfounded, the only words I could mutter were, "Best of luck, man." Jarret left without a pack and only a small, insulated pouch with what I assumed was his water. He was making great time and continued to blaze upward. Jarret never lacked stamina or strength. *"If you want to go fast, go alone."* However, climbing Denali without a rope team is not only forbidden by the National Park Service without an extensive approval process, but incredibly foolish, as one small misstep and you're likely to be part of Ranger Rick's next PowerPoint presentation.

As we moved slowly up the mountain over the next few hours, we saw the solo figure again, only this time coming down. Jarret had reached the summit. "Congrats, man! How was it? Did you snap some pictures?" We asked. "Nah, I only need mental photos."

We continued to climb until we reached that wonderful place where there was no more mountain to climb. Summits are always sweet. But the realization that we were only halfway done set in. We passed Luke and Cecil on the way down—fatigued, they left their packs below Pig Hill, the final section before the summit. They would later find that Jarret had drunk their much-needed liter of water they saved in their pack to consume on the return.

After we were all safely back at High Camp, we crashed and fell into a slumber, our entire group of six reaching the summit of North America, albeit our group arriving back at three different times of the day.

The following morning, we headed down for a full push to the bottom with a small break at the 14k Camp.

While climbing down the 800-foot descent of the Head Wall, the snow began to sluff from the consolidation of the overnight storm, creating uncertain footing and uneasy climbing. Jarret was supposed to wait for his rope team member, Luke, who was still down-climbing the fixed lines. Jarret jumped in with Cecil and Brandon and said he was heading back to 14k camp. Without warning, and before Tom and I could realize what was going on, Jarret took off for a safe retreat and left us on the side of the Head Wall with snow calving around us, waiting for Luke.

When we began to think about what just happened—that Jarret didn't want to wait for his rope mate, again, leaving us to break apart our trio—Tom had all but lost his patience. Since first meeting Tom my junior year of high school to this day, I have never seen him lose his temper—except once: that day on Denali. He was boiling over, and by the time we roped together with Luke and made it into camp, Tom had a full head of steam. Tom threw down his gear, marched over to Jarret, and said, "That's a bullshit move, dude." I'd also never heard Tom swear in our nearly three decades of friendship. Jarret, not one to take an attack sitting down, jumped up to be chin to chest with Tom and defended his position with equal fire. The barbs and verbal attacks flew fast and frequent between the two, although Jarret had no position to argue other than his desire to get into camp to rest and not having the patience to wait for his teammate, whom he'd been frustrated with for two straight weeks. When no one came to Jarret's aid (as if any of us would), he retreated in defeat and sunk inside his tent.

The remainder of the day the rest of us spent relaxing, basking in the well-deserved summit. Cecil and Tom somehow created a delicious fondue with cheddar cheese on bagels. How they produced such a culinary delight while snow flurried in an open-air kitchen is one of the greatest mountain marvels I have ever witnessed.

After a quick nap, we began packing up at 10 p.m. With return bush flights not landing until morning, there was no rush nor motivation to get down other than the bitter cold at our current camp. Around 3 a.m., we set out for the eight hours of down climbing. We were waiting for the Seattle guys to lead when there was a slight issue with Luke's bootlace. Jarret began his usual complaints and suggestions when, alas, on the final day, Luke's patience also reached his tipping point and he could take no more. Luke stood up, his 6 foot 5 inch frame towering over Jarret's 5 feet 8 inches, calmly looked down, and said simply and deliberately, "You Are a Fucking Asshole, You Know That?"

Tired of this dynamic, I let them know we were going ahead, and we set off. After a few hours of climbing down, the mountain that had been shrouded in clouds on our ascent now sprawled clearly open before us, exposing new peaks we had never seen. It's this beauty that hypnotized Denali's first mountaineers and continues to draw them in today. For me, outside the Himalayas, Denali is the most beautiful mountain range on this earth.

After loading our bush plane and landing back in Talkeetna in an attempt to catch our scheduled flight, we had a two-hour van ride where Jarret sat in complete silence. Tom, Brandon, and I boarded our redeye back to Salt Lake City and the Seattle crew spent the night in separate places.

A month and a half later, I received a 4-page email from Jarret filled with complaints about our expedition that were packaged as "helpful insights" for our future expeditions.

Among these "insights" were: that we didn't understand the importance of having an experienced leader to make decisions for the group instead of a having a democracy where "all voices were equally valid"; that we were a passive group who underreacted to a team member who was obviously in trouble and should not have been allowed to continue up the mountain (even though Luke summited and returned in good shape); that not being able to tell the difference between real hazards and imagined hazards, we ignored the real hazards and worried about the imagined ones; and that there was a general unwillingness of the team to appreciate Jarret's knowledge and experience, which led to his blow-up with Tom.

In my much shorter response to Jarret, I told him that I was sorry he felt our team was passive in decision-making, but noted that:

The groups I form and prefer to climb with have a relaxed vibe which shouldn't be confused with carelessness or recklessness. I've always felt a democratic style of climbing with my friends is a good way to make the expedition an enjoyable one and that the group's correct decision always surfaces and we're good with it.

As far as the Tom explosion, I can't speak for others, but it appeared to be an argument between two grown men that resolved itself.

I wish you all the best on your future summits!

That was the last I ever communicated with Jarret. It was the last anyone of us spoke with Jarret. Last I heard, he's moved and is no longer in the Seattle area. I do wish him all the best on his future summits, but it certainly won't be on my rope team.

THE IMPORTANCE OF THE TEAM

In sports, we tend to think in terms of individual sports, such as golf and tennis, and team sports, such as football and soccer. But whether their discipline is a team or an individual sport, the truth is that there is not a single professional athlete who is not a member of a dedicated team. Achieving success at the highest levels of sports is impossible without a strong, efficient, and effective team behind you. And the same holds true for any challenge that you might face or any quest on which you might embark. Your success, especially when you need to persist in the face of hardships or setbacks, depends in large part on the people you have on what I call your "rope team." They are the ones who arrest you if you fall, they are the ones who encourage you to continue, they are the ones who help you make the right decisions as you forge up the mountain.

However, if you have the wrong people tied into your rope team, you could be pulling dead weight or fighting an uphill battle even when going down the mountain.

FUNCTIONAL SYNERGY

In this chapter, I've been talking about choosing the right people for your team. But I like the following story because it shows just what a difference having the right people around you can make whether or not you chose them. This is a true story about a problem on an airplane—and how the right person with the right skills made the difference between life and death.

Thomas was a 30-year-old diabetic from Holland who, when he boarded a flight from Geneva to New Delhi, discovered that he had lost his insulin pump required for injecting insulin. He decided to attempt the flight, hoping that his blood sugar would remain low enough until his arrival. It was almost a fatal mistake. Thomas went into a hyperglycemic episode and needed an immediate injection of his insulin. At first, it seemed that luck would save him: there was a doctor on board, and the doctor happened to be diabetic himself, so he had insulin with him, as well as an injection pump, also known as a "pen."

Unfortunately, the doctor's insulin pen was made for a different type of insulin cartridge—one that administered long-term insulin very slowly. Thomas needed an injection of his fast-acting insulin. The plane decided to make an emergency landing, but as Thomas fell unconscious and started foaming at the mouth, the doctor knew that he would probably be dead by the time the plane landed. But there was nothing the doctor could do. He had the wrong injection pen needed to inject the right kind of insulin. He explained to the other passengers, hoping that perhaps another diabetic passenger might be present with the right pen.

At that point, a 21-year-old engineering student approached the doctor and asked if he could try to modify the doctor's pen to take Thomas's cartridge. He was able to change the holding tube diameter on the doctor's cartridge, but the needle wouldn't move. After downloading from the plane's Wi-Fi a design of the cartridge, the student realized a spring was missing, which was causing the problem. The student collected normal writing pens from the passengers, found one that fit the insulin cartridge and inserted it. The doctor's reconfigured pen now worked, and the doctor was able to inject Thomas's insulin into Thomas. Within 15 minutes, Thomas regained consciousness and the danger passed.

The skills of a doctor are often called on in sudden medical emergencies, but in this case, those skills alone would not have been enough to save Thomas. The lesson of this story for me is that nothing beats *complementary* skills. In this case, an engineer and a doctor teamed up to save a life, and only the two of them together could have done it. Our Kilimanjaro and safari company would not be possible without my business partner, Nickson, effectively doing what he does best in fulfilling the operational side of trekking and safaris; at the same time, our company would not have the number of clients we have without the knowledge, marketing, and client acquisition efforts of myself and my wife.

Perhaps one of the most important guidelines in choosing your rope team is to surround yourself with people from different backgrounds, with different and complementary experiences and skills. While Jarret's personality clashed with nearly everyone in our group, and his constant tips on mountaineering were often discarded, I still appreciated his take on our situation, his look at the mountain, his concern on the stability of snowpack, and techniques on how to down climb. If nothing else, it caused pause to double check our own ideas and ensure we were making the right choices. The challenges you face will not always be the same. It's true that if you are an actor trying to make it in Hollywood, or you are a salesman trying to exceed quota, you will benefit from the experience of those who are in your field. But as an aspiring actor, you might be surprised by what a salesperson could teach you about succeeding in auditions. After all, salespeople are auditioning every day. And as a salesperson, you might be surprised by what an actor could teach you about presenting your best self and connecting with a prospect. After all, actors are selling in their own way every day, selling their acting gifts, selling the authenticity of their characters.

Don't limit your network. Whatever your question, don't go for the obvious team members. The more complementary and diverse the skills on your rope team, the greater chance you, like Thomas, have of surviving.

PSYCHOLOGICAL SYNERGY

For business psychologist Dave Winsborough, author of *Fusion: The Psychology of Teams*, having the right mix of *personalities* on a team is as important as having the right mix of functional skills. For Winsborough, every person on a team has two roles—a functional role and a psychological role—and most team leaders focus on the functional skills and assume those are enough to ensure that the team can work together well.

As you are thinking of the people who will help you reach your summits, keep both of each person's roles in mind. Although there are personalities that you will find easier to work with, to put together the most effective rope team that will help you through any challenge, seek out different, complementary personalities just as you seek out different, complementary functions.

Through his work, Winsborough has identified five distinct personalities that together create the psychological synergy essential for effective teams. Here are Winsborough's five personalities, with the names of the people from my Denali rope team who displayed the personalities, and my take on how each personality can help you achieve your goals:

[Me] Results-oriented. These types of people have the energy and focus to get things done. As advisors, they will keep you focused on the prize.

[Cecil and Tom] Relationship-focused. These are the people who know how to build and nurture relationships. They are an important counterpoint to the results-oriented personalities, often helping to tone down their relentless, sometimes scorched-earth drive through diplomacy. As advisors they will help you develop the relationships you need to achieve your goals.

[Jarret] Process and rule-followers. The devil can be in the details and these kinds of personalities pay attention to the details. When you're faced with a challenge or a setback, you may react with broad strokes, either negatively or positively. The grounded, usually unflappable process and rule-followers, which Winsborough describes as "reliable, organized, and conscientious," will surface the details that you might sweep away in the energy of the moment.

[Luke] Innovative and disruptive thinkers. You might be stuck, frustrated that you're not where you want to be, or angry at yet another setback. Perhaps one of the most valuable personalities to help you through the hard times is the innovative or disruptive thinker, who comes up with an idea or plan that is completely off your radar and that might, at first, seem ridiculous or unachievable. But in the end, it may be the plan that works.

[Brandon] Pragmatic. The counterpoint to the disruptive thinker is the relentlessly pragmatic member of your team, who will offer you caution and emotional stability. They might not be enthusiastic advocates of persistence in the face of daunting challenges—let the results-oriented and innovative personalities on your team help you with that—but they will help you succeed in your persistence with grounded advice like, "We keep going when all others turned back."

Winsborough, a New Zealander who founded a large business psychology-based practice in New Zealand and now works with Hogan Assessments, has worked with numerous teams around the world who offer specific examples of the value of these five personalities. He describes, for example a finance team that failed in its mission to change the financial reporting culture of a government agency. As quoted in a *Harvard Business Review* article, the following percentage of players in each of the five personality categories above doomed the team from the start:

- results-oriented: 17% of team members

- relationship builders: 0% of team members

- process-oriented: 50% of team members

- innovative or disruptive thinkers: 0% of team members

- pragmatic: 100% of team members

Not a single person on the team above was good at building relationships. How can you help an organization change its culture if you are not building relationships with any members of that organization? The under-representation of result-oriented people was another disadvantage for this team, which, indeed, failed to get results.

Another team studied by Winsborough included *too many* relationship-builders, and once again, no results-oriented members. The personalities of this team were distributed as follows:

- results-oriented: 0% of team members

- relationship builders: 86% of team members

- process-oriented: 29% of team members

- innovative or disruptive thinkers: 29% of team members

- pragmatic: 0% of team members

One can imagine the challenges of this team. There was much cohesion and harmony... and nothing got done.

Winsborough's figures illustrate why psychological synergy is important for your rope team, although I wouldn't spend too much time developing a percentage breakdown of the people who are advising and influencing you. Instead, ask yourself, for each of these five personalities, do you have at least one influential person in your life who embodies that personality?

SOMETIMES YOU'VE GOT TO CUT THE ROPE

Each one of us has a member of the team who continuously drags us down, who continuously seeks out the worst and most dangerous element in any situation and starts ringing the alarm bell. And here's the problem: there is no way to cut this person off the rope team because this person is *you*! Or, more specifically, your brain, which is hardwired to seek out the negative and warn us. Of course, it's not the brain's fault—or to be even more specific, it's not the amygdala's fault—because the amygdala is that part of the brain that is given a specific responsibility: to help us survive. It's the amygdala that helps us notice the 30-foot ice serac leaning in a way that could fall on you or on your path, or that strange smell when your tent door is on fire because Tom didn't pay attention to the windy tent flap as he was boiling water for dinner! As for that beautiful clear sky above the serac or the promise of a delicious freeze-dried pasta primavera, the amygdala's not interested.

The bottom line: we are hardwired to be negative. It's where our biology takes us. And that's why having negative people around can be so destructive, because their negativity confirms what our brain wants to tell us. In the words of psychologist Matthew James, "our brain will chew on that negativity like a dog with a favorite bone. We'll even feel a kind of satisfaction as we do it—because our primitive brain is telling us that this focus is making us safe."

If psychologically we're hardwired to be negative, then we have to psychologically work at building what James calls our "immune system" against negativity and negative people. One way to build up this psychological immune system is to get rid of emotional baggage. If negative people clip onto your rope, it's because they often reflect the emotional baggage that you may be carrying. If you're recovering from a bad relationship, hearing someone complain about his or her relationship is going to send you spiraling down into unhappiness. The negative people are talking about their problems, but it's your problem that is being revived. Persistence requires strength that is not zapped by lingering emotional baggage.

James also suggests "reframing," which is to deliberately try to see something from another way. When dealing with negative people, this could mean deliberately rejecting their half-empty take on something.

Are negative people still pulling you in? If so, here are two more suggestions from James. First, talk to them, tell them that you respect their opinion, but that's not how you feel and that's not what you want to listen to. The last suggestion? *Cut the rope.* You have to make choices, he says. I have decided, for example, that I limit the negative news feeds I allow into my mobile devices. News is overwhelmingly negative, and I decided to cut out that negativity. On social media I hide my obnoxious friends who continue to voice their ineffectual political opinions.

You could argue there's some irresponsibility as a citizen in not watching any news whatsoever. I have international businesses that are dependent on what's happening with the safety of the countries I operate. I ensure that I am aware of and had marketing and messaging to respond to the Ebola outbreak in 2014 and the Corona virus in 2020. But I made the choice for negative media, and that's my point: make a deliberate choice to refuse negative people on your rope team.

TRUE NORTH GROUPS: BILL GEORGE'S ROPE TEAM

Every Wednesday morning, between 7:15 a.m. and 8:30 a.m., Bill George, former CEO of Medtronic and author of *Authentic Leadership* and *True North*, meets with what he calls his True North Group, a small group of friends who discuss openly and confidentially among themselves their professional and personal issues and challenges. When his wife was diagnosed with cancer, George credits his True North Group with helping him overcome his denial about his wife's condition—a denial caused in part by his history with the disease, which had already killed his mother and his fiancée.

George is such a believer of these types of open, confidential, and honest groups, he's created a seminar for Harvard built around True North Groups, and co-authored a book about them. This is how he describes True North groups in the book: "These groups provide a safe, confidential place where people can share their experiences, challenges, and frustrations and get honest feedback … At various times, a True North Group functions as a nurturer, a grounding rod, a truth teller, and a mirror. At their best, members serve each other as caring coaches and thoughtful mentors."

For me, True North Groups sound like ideal persistent rope teams, the kind that will help you hurdle the barriers that inevitably come up in life and set you straight if you wonder off the path.

Of course, groups of people helping each other or meeting for a favorite activity are not new. From book clubs to drug and alcohol rehabilitation support groups to personal boards of advisors, people come together to share ideas, offer support, and enjoy each other's company around a hobby. The difference with True North Groups, according to George, is that there is not a single common topic (e.g., alcohol dependency or shared religious beliefs or, in the case of personal boards of advisors, a focus on professional success). The topics are much more open and personal, designed only to help achieve what he calls one's *True North*—which can be generally summarized as success, whether professional or personal, based on one's deeply felt values and principles.

But you have to have the right people in your True North Group. And it's important not to compromise. A True North group will sink with just one or two people who shouldn't be there.

In the book, George lays out a plan for someone starting a True North Group, including a specific program for the first 12 sessions of the group. For example, the first session should be focused on sharing life stories and stories about the people who are most important to you or who had the greatest impact. In the second session, members of the group should talk about when they lost their way, perhaps by abandoning their values. And in the third session, members of the group should talk about the crucibles in their lives, the turning points in their lives and what lessons they learned from them.

What I like about George's True North Groups is that this is not some intellectual concept made up by a consultant to sell. George began meeting his True North group every Wednesday morning 36 years ago—and they continue uninterrupted today.

While you probably don't need an organizational chart for your rope team, identifying who you want to include, writing out their "role"—how they can help you succeed—and listing specific ways that they can fulfill their roles—their "responsibilities to you" will help you focus on a core group of people whom you can turn to for advice and guidance when faced with setbacks and challenges but also when deciding how to react to opportunities. Because when you're tied together, you succeed, or you fail together.

CHAPTER FOUR

PREPARING YOUR PACK: THE POWER OF LOGISTICS

The line between disorder and order lies in logistics

– Sun Tzu

At 23,000 feet, it's common to have a restless night in Camp 3, hanging precariously on a ledge that has been chiseled out of the hard snow at the very center of Everest's Lhotse face (as far as possible from the avalanche-prone slopes that surround the camp). With the pending summit spiraling in our minds, we prepared our packs while oxygen seeped into our masks at 1/2 liter per minute. This was our summit bid. Today we would climb to our final stop, Camp 4, before resting, rehydrating, and making our assault on the top of the world later that evening. It was 3:30 a.m., and our guides were laboriously boiling snow to replenish the water in our bottles: two liters each that must last for the next 12 hours of punishing climbing. With every step and exhalation of breath, our bodies would lose valuable water, necessitating us to sip our depleting water supply regularly. The tireless Sherpas provided a barely edible bowl of spicy tomato soup and broken noodles for our breakfast; not only does every ounce count in what you put in your pack, but every ounce counts in what you put in your stomach, so we choked it down.

This is not the time to forget something—food, drink, oxygen, equipment, or anything else that we needed for the final push. Despite my fatigue, the cold, and breathing through the cumbersome oxygen mask, I focused all my attention on what I would carry in my pack. Ultimately, my pack included a sleeping mat for our brief rest at Camp 4, extra expedition socks, a small yellow waterproof journal and pen, camera with batteries, expedition weight gloves and mittens, balaclava, extra cap, glove liners, expedition weight base layer, GPS tracker, sunglasses, lip balm, sunscreen, goggles with clear and polarized lenses, 16 oz. small-mouth water bottle for inside my summit suit, three liquid energy gels, six Snickers bars, summit banners, a laminated photo of my niece, Gracie, who passed away at the tender age of one and the laminated 2x3 picture of my family that has been with me on every step of Everest. A pack full of items, all imperative; nothing more, nothing less. At 5:30 a.m., we suited up, crampons fixed and the oxygen flow increased to 1.5 liters per minute, and set off to climb the second half of the Lhotse face and beyond.

We were barely 15 minutes into our climb, only 100 feet above Camp 3, when we came upon a lethargic climber slumped on a ledge adjacent to the fixed lines we were ascending. He appeared to be completely incapacitated. I knelt over his bent body and gently asked him his name. My question went unanswered. He didn't acknowledge my presence, nor did his eyes shift focus; they just stared blankly through mine. Unlike everyone else on the mountain, he wasn't wearing a one-piece high altitude summit suit.

Instead, he wore a blue expedition parka and pants. He wasn't even carrying oxygen and appeared to be climbing alone without a guide. It was evident that he had been out all night or at least on the ledge for an extended period of time. One hand still retained a mitten but the other was bare, completely exposed to the elements. His gloveless hand was waxy white, the sign that frostbite had set in long ago. I attempted to put his hand back into his jacket sleeve and place it under his armpit. In his stupor, he kept pulling it back out. I rubbed his back and let him know help was coming. Our team stayed close, I pulled my oxygen mask to the side and yelled down to the camp below, "He needs a rescue; he needs oxygen!" I repeated this two more times. Possibly the most startling discovery was what was— or rather was *not*—in his backpack. We looked inside to find nothing but a thermos. This climber was totally unprepared on a mountain that requires absolute preparation.

Other climbers soon joined us and assessed his condition as well. It's a helpless feeling being in a situation where you want nothing more than to help someone, and being completely incapable of providing them aid. On Everest, descending with an incapacitated climber is incredibly difficult and dangerous, and is often impossible. The Sherpa guides who have trained in this type of rescue are the only ones I've seen successfully accomplish this. A U.S. climbing guide right behind me radioed into basecamp providing exact details of the situation and a description of the climber: "There's a climber in a blue jacket in bad shape. Likely European." "Copy that." With nothing more we could do; we continued our climb. I would look back every few minutes. Each climber that followed was checking on him as well. After climbing about 45 minutes, the route turned over a ridge where he was no longer in my sight. I would find out the following day that within an hour of passing him, Russian Rustem Amirov had died. Sherpas had come to provide oxygen, but it was too late.

Rustem's fate played out long before he stepped foot on Everest. Several errors in judgment contributed to his tragic end; multiple, seemingly insignificant, poor decisions all accruing, and ultimately, leading to his incongruous death. From what I later gathered, Rustem attempted to purchase a permit to climb Everest, but upon arrival in Kathmandu to begin his expedition, he realized the company he had contracted with was fraudulent and nowhere to be found. Undeterred and still wanting to climb something in the Himalayas, he was able to secure a permit to climb Lhotse. The Lhotse climbing route follows the Everest south side route to a spot called the Yellow Band, a ribbon of yellow limestone that cuts across Everest and Lhotse, just above Camp 3. At that point, the two routes diverge, with the Lhotse route climbing the couloir about a mile and a half south of Everest's summit. Lhotse is only 1,000 feet lower in elevation than Everest and is a challenging climb that is not to be underestimated.

Rustem didn't arrive in base camp until early May, a late start. On May 16, Maxut Zhumayev, a mountain guide from Kazakhstan, was on his way up to Camp 4 when he passed Rustem near the Yellow Band. He recognized Rustem as they had become acquaintances while in base camp. According to Zhumayev,

Rustem was going very slowly, and I thought he was very tired, and I first thought he was on the mountain and now he's going down. We met and got to talking, and he told me he had a very hard night (headache, cough), and with another climber were very slow speed, he realized that they had to get down the mountain. In this extreme moment, I did not specify whether he had tried or not, the main thing I noted was that his hands were shaking, he was very tired. I gave him a full cup of thermos hot water and made him eat one tile waffle, explaining it was a bit of glucose, and he needed strength to go down to the base camp for rest.

We talked, and I explained how important it is to lose altitude right now. I told him that strong fatigue was setting in, I myself have been in a situation where I am very tired at altitude. I knew that Rustem had to come down, so I wished him luck again, we continued up and he went down. Once again, I looked at Rustem from the top of the Yellow Band. He was slow, but he was going down.

The next time Maxut would see Rustem was two days later upon his return to Camp 3. He saw a dead climber with his boots sticking out of a tent. At first, he didn't know those boots were Rustem's, only that the Camp managers were talking and didn't know what to do with this unattended body, as no one was claiming responsibility for the cost to reclaim him. It was sorted out within a few days, and his body was eventually returned to his wife.

Four days before his death, Rustem posted on Facebook, "The weather data has moved to 16 May to match my plans, the American team in the neighborhood is also oriented on the dates of May 16-17, but they go to Everest." We were the American team to which he was referring. He finished his post with, "Send me away and wait for news in a week!"

I will carry the look Rustem gave me—his glassy eyes staring through mine—for the rest of my days. Severe cerebral edema had caused swelling on his brain, with a buildup of fluid, to the point of no recovery. I will also carry the lessons of two very different approaches to our respective summit ambitions. As legendary U.S. mountaineer Ed Viesturs has said, "Getting to the top is optional. Getting down is mandatory."

THE ELEMENTS OF LOGISTICS

Logistics is making sure that we have the necessary resources to achieve our summits. When setting out to conquer whatever is on our horizon, how often do we start with an empty pack? How many times do we not take life-sustaining oxygen? How many times do we go it alone without a guide who's climbed the route before us? How many times do we not bring the nutritional resources required to keep us functioning? Companies spend millions screening applicants, acquiring new talent, and putting in place training programs, but neglect to provide the resources for success in the field once hired.

When preparing for expeditions with my group, I think that I, at times, annoy my friends with shared Google docs, conference calls, route reviews, endless contingency planning for various scenarios (weather, injured climber, failing equipment, etc.), travel arrangements, and itinerary. Every detail from the daily start times to the last dried mango slice is pre-planned. The result is that every expedition, on every peak, has been organized to perfection—which is why our expeditions to Denali, Aconcagua, Elbrus, and Vinson were successful even when they necessitated adjustments for poor weather, ill climbers, or various equipment issues. Simply put, we were prepared and anticipated all these complications and thus, reached the summits.

I recognized from my very first failed training hike up King's Peak, the highest peak in Utah, that if you don't pay attention to the logistics of the expedition, your expedition will likely fail. And for high altitude expeditions such as the ones involved in climbing the Seven Summits, failure can be a question of life or death. That's the importance of logistics.

So, what exactly is logistics? As I mentioned, logistics in climbing is ensuring that you have the right resources—the right equipment, the right tools, and the right amount of food, water, oxygen, and any other resource that you will or might need—to enjoy the expedition, to be as safe as possible, and to succeed in the most cost-effective and efficient way possible. (Managing costs is an important component of successful logistics).

It's important to emphasize that logistics is not just about supply and equipment. It's about *people*. If you think about it, an expedition could be described as a series of ongoing interactions between people and other people (your rope team, other climbers on the mountain) and between people and nature (the mountain and the weather). Those interactions can be positive or negative. Climbers will come to the aid of other climbers, but there can be clashes among climbers. Nature can "smile" on your expedition or unleash its fatal fury.

The job of logistics is to make sure that the people on the expedition are moving forward and safe.

At the heart of all logistics is a *plan*. This is absolutely critical. And we're talking about a plan—not a scenario, not a wish list, not an exciting dream, but a plan that covers in minute and exhaustive *detail* every facet of the expedition. There is no element or no contingency that must be ignored. For example, one often-overlooked item of expedition logistical planning is the decision-making process: who will make the decisions when there are alternative approaches or responses to consider? Will you leave it all to your guide and will you listen and obey his or her final decision? On our failed attempt on Everest, we deliberated for 20 minutes on the South Summit trying to convince our lead guide, Sarki, that our physical strength was mightier than Mother Nature.

Mountain expeditions involve interactions between and among people and nature. People and weather are dynamic elements. The logistics plan has to take into account the strengths and weaknesses of the people involved (the schedule, for example, must be doable) and the fact that these strengths and weaknesses might fluctuate (a strong climber like Tom was suddenly dealing with unanticipated serious stomach bug he caught on our trek into Everest Base Camp). The same holds true for nature, such as the weather, which may suddenly and unexpectedly change.

In short, the most important characteristic of a logistics plan is *flexibility*. The plan must be built around anticipation and adaptation: You develop a plan that anticipates what is going to happen and fallback plans that allow you to adapt if necessary. By my very nature of planning everything down to a T, I'm typically inflexible.

Another important characteristic of logistics planning is *efficiency*. You need to have enough food and equipment to cover all contingencies and emergencies, while at the same time you cannot bring too much food and too much equipment to the mountain, as every ounce counts, and any additional weight compounds each step and increases fatigue.

There is a similar balance between too little and too much that must be achieved in terms of effort. You must be prepared to put in the time and effort required for both planning—which can take years!—and for the actual expedition itself. This balance can be achieved by the careful allocation of your effort, and by that I mean not only how much effort you put into the expedition-related planning and tasks, but also when you put in that effort. Just as on the mountain there is a time to push forward relentlessly and there is a time to rest, in the logistical planning of the expedition, there is also a time when you need to rest and regroup—otherwise, you will be burnt out.

SEVEN LESSONS FOR LOGISTICAL PLANNING

Based on the discussion above, we can draw out some key lessons about logistical planning.

1) Summit before you summit: acquire the knowledge you need to succeed.

During my pursuit of the Seven Summits, the first thing that I always did after deciding on the next summit was to learn everything I could about the mountain: optimal summit *day*, not month or week, but actual calendar summit day, permit costs, the route up the mountain, weather conditions, potential political and regulatory restrictions, rope team for this particular mountain, time off work, and vetting the guide. For our Denali expedition, I studied a guide, Brent Okita, who had summited an impressive 20 straight years with his clients. In 2014, I looked at his itinerary and determined the day he planned to summit. He knew something I didn't. I planned our summit window to mirror his, and June 4th was his expected summit day. Even though we climbed in the worst weather in four decades, we summited, and passed Brent Okita with his group on the way down. He didn't know me, but on our way down I congratulated him on his new summit record, and *I* told *him* thanks. He had no idea what I meant. If you're going to plan every expedition like I did, it's all on you. I didn't have the financial resources when I first started climbing to afford the ease of signing up for a commercially guided group of strangers. No, I had to figure it all out. I would summit each mountain dozens of times in my mind, in the gym, in books, and often in some obscure version in my dreams long before I stepped foot on the actual mountain. I would go to bed after researching the Western Buttress route on Denali and find myself repeatedly climbing just short of the summit with my climbing partner Brandon. I remember one dream reaching the top and thinking it was much easier than I thought—in reality it was exactly the opposite! Obviously, for my initial expedition, I first had to acquire the mountain-climbing knowledge and skill set needed to survive on Mt. Rainier.

2) Set up camps along the way: establish milestones.

When I speak to corporations or local groups about climbing, I sometime pose the question: what's the ultimate goal of a mountain expedition? It seems obvious, the crowd replies: reach the summit. Understandable answer. But I tell them returning home with all your fingers and toes is the ultimate goal. But beneath that overarching goal are a number of key sequential milestones without which success is improbable. For example, in my climb to the summit of Aconcagua, we set to climb this mountain in two weeks—any commercially guided outfit takes three weeks. Our milestones had to be aggressive: reaching the mountain the following day after flying into Mendoza. Reaching Camp 2, Nido de Condores within 7 days of starting our expedition, and ending up at the final Camp 3, Camp Colera (the final high camp), the day before our summit day so we'd have an extra poor weather day if needed. Which we did need and which we used to perfection.

3) The devil is in the details.

The difference between reaching the summit or even returning alive from the mountain often comes down to details. For example, you don't just plan to have food and drink, you break down exactly what and how much you are going to eat and drink every meal and snack of the expedition. I'm continuously surprised by climbers who die on the mountain because they didn't think through how much hydration might be needed. I know through experience that when I use a hydration bladder, each sip is about 1 ounce. With a 2-liter bladder, I have about sixty sips. By taking a few sips each 15 minutes during a trek or climb, I know exactly when I'm going to run out of liquid and know how to ration accordingly.

4) Back up the back up: make contingency plans.

Related to focusing on the details is the importance of making contingency plans. If you just have one rigid plan for reaching the summit, chances are you are going to fail because neither human beings nor nature are completely predictable. You have to plan for the unexpected.

5) Identify and acquire the right resources.

If you skimp on equipment and materials on the mountain, or don't know what you really need, you are going to fail. Remember, I was amazed by what I did *not* find in Rustem's pack.

When I first started climbing in my late 20's, I couldn't afford the proper quality gear. I bought used equipment on eBay such as purple Koflach mountaineering boots, aluminum crampons, and an ice axe that was too short. On those purple boots, which could have been the original mountaineering boots ever made, the foam was brittle and ended up cold and cracked. The aluminum crampons dulled and scarred easily on any rock, and my short ice axe length kept me leaning too far into the mountain. Repurchasing La Sportiva boots, steel crampons and a 70 cm length axe made all the difference. At the same time, don't go overboard. Don't weigh yourself down with just-in-case equipment that you will never use.

6) Have a realistic picture of how much effort you can expend.

Unfortunately, there are no qualification procedures for mountain climbing outside the United States, unlike, for example, prequalification's for major marathons. Anyone can attempt to climb Mt. Everest, even if they have no idea of what physical capabilities are required. There are countless stories of the people who die on big mountains who never should have been there in the first place and in so doing, endanger others around them.

7) Have a realistic picture of how much time you need.

This is perhaps the most crucial consideration in mountain climbing planning, and it is linked to all of the other principles, including the importance of details, making contingency plans, and acquiring the right resources. On the mountain we talk about a "summit window" because that is one of the fundamental constraints of mountain climbing: you are going to have a limited time to succeed. Which means that you better manage that time perfectly—and even if you do that, your schedule is probably going to be knocked around a bit by new developments.

Time management off the mountain is often a question of productivity, getting things done, achieving what you want to achieve. On the mountain, time management can be the difference between life and death. Mismanage time, climb too slow, or ignore your turn around time, and there's an increased chance of disaster.

PLANNING FOR PERSISTENCE: DAY-TO-DAY LOGISTICS FOR *YOUR* SUMMIT

As with mountain expeditions, any pursuit in life requires logistics. Any goal that you are trying to achieve requires logistics, even if you've never used that term before. Think about the logistics of acquiring a traditional college degree. You need the required books and other tools, you need a place to sleep, you need access to food, access to the library, and other learning resources—all of which comprise logistics. And these details are not unimportant, which is why, especially for underclassmen, universities provide housing, meals, and a college bookstore.

One of the constraints, but also an advantage, of reaching a summit is that it is not an open opportunity. You will only have a certain amount of time to touch the top, that summit window, and if you can't, you have to get off the mountain.

A long-term life goal might require months or even years of persistence. How can logistics help you achieve such a goal? In this case, the most important contribution of logistics is to help you progress every day, day-after-day, week-after-week, and year-to-year. This is what I call Planning for Persistence. It's establishing a logistical plan for your goal, whether that goal is in six weeks, six months, or six years.

The seven lessons of logistical planning that applied to mountain climbing apply equally to the pursuit of any ambitious goals, whether it's to give a public presentation or learn a new language, to launch a successful business, to reach C-suite in your company, or whatever else you may be pursuing.

We do have to add one more lesson, and that's the one we begin with: "Know your summits."

KNOW YOUR SUMMITS

The beauty of mountain climbing is that it is always driven by a clear-cut and simple goal: reach the summit and return. There aren't many human endeavors in which the goals are so clearly defined. Many people never reach their summits for the simple reason that they never defined them in the first place. For instance, people will spend more time studying their weekly fantasy football picks than studying their money.

How does this apply to logistics? Simple. Imagine an expedition team gathering around the table. They're confirming that the expedition members have all of the equipment and food and contingency plans to reach the summit. Suddenly, someone asks, "Wait, does anyone know which mountain we're climbing?" Blank stares and shrugs around the table. It never occurred to anyone in the group to figure out which mountain they were climbing, so everyone gets up and goes home... because logistical planning is impossible if you don't know the goal.

That, of course, would never happen with mountaineers. But if I asked you, what is your plan for increasing your net worth by $20,000 before New Year's Eve, would you be able to answer? And would it be a clear number and with an exact date? If you don't have a set financial, physical, or mental health plan, it just doesn't happen. The man on top of the mountain didn't fall there—said Vince Lombardi. I have a monthly calendar reminder on the first day of the month at 10:00 a.m., no matter where I am in the world, to update my financials, resulting in an accurate net worth. I update a Google Spreadsheet with each stock portfolio, rental property balances, business net profit balances, and other real estate ventures. It takes the same amount of time as updating fantasy picks and provides a much more meaningful concept of how your financial team is doing. By now, you are probably familiar with the often-used concept of SMART goals. SMART stands for Specific, Measurable, Attainable, Relevant, and Time-bound. These are good guidelines for defining your goal, but they are not the only ones.

Two of the pioneers of goal theory are perhaps being shouted over by all the goal gurus crowding the bookshelves and motivational conferences today, but I believe their work, based on decades of academic research and produced long before SMART goals became ubiquitous, stands the test of time. The two pioneers are Dr. Edwin Locke of the University of Maryland and Dr. Gary Latham of the University of Toronto. In 1968, Locke laid out the importance of goal setting in his important *Organizational Behavior and Human Performance* article, "Toward a Theory of Task Motivation and Incentives." Locke's contention was that whether incentives such as monetary incentives, time limits, competition, praise or reproach were effective depended a great deal on the goals and intentions of individuals. But not just any goals: Locke's research showed that the goals that people really worked hard to achieve were *specific* and *challenging*—one of the first to question the effectiveness of general, "Do your best" goals. Latham's research at Toronto's Rotman School of Management supported Locke's conclusions about goals, and in 1990, the two collaborated on the groundbreaking book, *A Theory of Goal Setting and Task Performance.*

The book set out five principles of goal setting, the first two being *clarity* (related to Latham's "specific" attribute) and *challenge*, with three new principles of *commitment, feedback* and *task complexity*. Commitment means that you are rationally and emotionally committed to the goal. Feedback means that you are monitoring your progress towards the goal (or having your progress monitored). Goals may need to be adjusted over time. And task complexity involves the complexity of the goal. Goals that are too complex are not likely to be achieved.

In many ways, Clarity, Challenge, Commitment, Feedback, and Complexity are principles that perfectly define the goal of reaching a mountain summit (although they will apply to any goal that requires persistence):

Clarity: The summit.

Challenge: The climb across brutal terrain often in brutal weather. The trail to the top is never smooth.

Commitment: You don't reach the summit without a total physical and mental commitment to the goal.

Feedback: Every step of the way, you know your progress—or lack of progress.

Complexity: Reaching the summit is difficult enough. Don't make it any harder than it needs to be.

ACQUIRE THE KNOWLEDGE YOU NEED TO SUCCEED

Once you have the goal—the summit that is at the end of your pursuit—you can use the seven lessons of logistical planning to help you reach that summit. The first of the seven lessons was to *acquire the knowledge you need to succeed.* No serious mountaineer would start up the mountain without knowing what lies above them. Yet too many of us rarely take the time to research our goal: What does it take to succeed as an entrepreneur? How have other people done it? No matter what your goal, learn everything you can about what stands between where you are now and the summit.

If your goal is to work for the diplomatic corps someday, what are the requirements and prerequisites for a job in the State Department? If you want to move to Paris to paint, what visas and other documents do you need to turn this dream into a reality? Is it possible to work remotely?

My grade school girlfriend Natalie's dad was a professional racecar driver. One show and tell, he came cruising around to the back of the school, revving his engine. He jumped out of the window and called me up. He placed his racer helmet on my kindergarten body, and I thought it was the best day of my life. Right there, I wanted to be a racecar driver.

Intuitively, you will know some of the requirements to become successful in this highly competitive field. The first is incredible driving skill and courage. The second is that you'll have to climb the ladder—and the younger you start, the better. Many professional racers start with karting in their pre-teen years to hone their racing skills (before the legal driving age), then move on to bigger and bigger cars (e.g., midget cars and sprint cars). As with most sports, it's difficult to reach professional level if you are starting a serious career after your teens.

But perhaps one of the greatest barriers to success is that racing costs money—and a lot of it. Long before you'll get anywhere near the top or even mid-tier levels of the sport, you will have to pay for the cars, the mechanics, the racing fees, and everything else. Which, unless you're independently wealthy, means finding someone to foot these bills. Becoming a racecar driver means launching a business, with you as the product. Are you prepared to spend years selling yourself to investors? I was not, and my ideas of driving fast cars have only led to more speeding tickets.

Whatever your goal, do your homework. Identify all the barriers and challenges that you will have to overcome. Only when you have that daunting list in front of you can you build an effective logistical plan.

ESTABLISH MILESTONES

Any journey or quest would be practically unbearable without milestones. The reason: milestones turn the mountain into smaller molehills.

Everest's Northeast route (Tibet) is often preferred by guides over the Southeast (Nepal) route because of the ease and safety of the route and also the ability to drive on a paved road all the way to base camp. But for the mountaineering purist, the Nepal side is often preferred, as you travel the 40-mile trek to base camp, immersing in the rich history of the Sherpa people along the way. You visit their sacred temples, stay in lodges at local villages called teahouses, pass sacred route markers called Stupas and visit memorials to fallen climbers along the way.

Once you've established a clear overall goal, the next step in planning for persistence is establishing the milestones. Whether your goal is to reach partner in the law firm, or to reach $10 million in sales, or to win the highest professional award in your field, there are always milestones that can be identified along the journey. Someone has come before you and shown the way. Identify them in your plan and be specific. Is there someone 10 years older than you in better physical shape? Is there someone 10 years younger than you who's achieved more financial success? You can learn from any walk of life.

And that's only the beginning. To be persistent, you have to force yourself to make progress every day. I'm a big believer in daily milestones or goals that push you forward throughout the day. I like to set up what I call my daily summit. I write down one thing that I want to accomplish and do it first thing. It doesn't have to be the biggest thing, it doesn't even have to be the smallest thing, it just has to be one thing that is absolutely mission critical. One day it could be updating a photo on my website, another day it would be making 15 sales calls, while another could be pushing another 5 minutes in a stair climbing workout. My daily summits are varied and unlimited. I don't check my team's box scores, and I don't check social media until that daily summit is reached.

Persisting in anything requires a continual, repeated structure. Setting daily milestones can instill that structure in your day-to-day activity.

FOCUS ON THE DETAILS

Logistics is about details. As described above, I know exactly how much hydration I have on my climbs and when that liquid will run out. On the mountain, dehydration can slow your pace, affect your judgment and even kill you. When you are planning for persistence, the more detail you can provide, the better. When tackling the obstacle of writing this book, if I wanted to succeed I'd have to go granular. How many hours a day am I going to write? What time of day am I writing? How many words do I want to reach per week? If you have a broader plan—to make a million dollars by the age of 30—your details will be broader. However, you still need to start from the summit and work down. Remember, a logistical plan is not a wish list. It lays out what you are going to do to get to where you want to be.

While the depth of details in a logistical plan will fit the objective of the plan, make sure that you have considered all the details related to what you want to achieve. Now is the time, when you are in the planning phase. When you're tied into the rope on the mountainside, the time to prepare has passed.

MAKE CONTINGENCY PLANS

Every effective logistical recipe has flexibility baked into it. Every contingency, every potential event is planned for. The same holds true for the logistics of your dream. Say your goal is to be C-level in your company in five years. One of your milestones is to get into an elite leadership development program, one in which the participants are chosen by their managers. But what if you don't get into that leadership development program? Do you abandon the dream? Flexibility in your plans will strengthen your persistence. Because if one door is suddenly blocked, you have three other doors through which you can push.

Hollywood producer and studio head Peter Guber enjoyed success in the movie industry at an early age. Recruited by Columbia Pictures out of law school, Guber would become Studio Chief within three years, leading Columbia to record profits. He would go on to form record companies (Casablanca Records, Polygram) and serve as Chairman and CEO of Sony Pictures before launching the Mandalay Entertainment Group, which now includes not only film and music ventures but also professional sports teams. Guber attributes his success "to being able to anticipate curve balls and turn them into home runs." As he writes in a LinkedIn article called "Career Curveball: The Uncertain Pitch Can Be Your Home Run," "considering the opportunities in your career as linear and predictable will limit your success at bat." To anticipate these curve balls, Guber decided to develop "transportable skills" that would allow him to move around the entertainment industry. Instead of fearing sudden setbacks, he started predicting and even "depending on" the curve balls to advance his career.

Sometimes, moving to a contingency plan can be the best thing to happen to you. Legendary investor Warren Buffett was intent on going to Harvard Business School and was confident that he would be accepted, and with good reason: even more important than being a recent University of Pennsylvania graduate, Buffett was already a successful businessperson, having earned $53,000 by the age of sixteen. Then the unthinkable happened: he was rejected by Harvard, which was unimpressed with his stock-picking skills. Buffett was undeterred. If Harvard wouldn't have him, he'd find another top business school to take him. Combing through catalogs, he noticed that Benjamin Graham, the author of *The Intelligent Investor*, taught at Columbia Business School. Buffett had read and admired Graham's book, and realized that Columbia offered him an opportunity to meet and hopefully be mentored by the master investor. In the Buffett biography *Snowball*, author Alice Shroeder quotes one of his roommates as saying, "It was like he had found a god." Being rejected by Harvard turned out to be a life-changing moment for Warren Buffett. Our greatest pains lead to our greatest change.

It's important to make the distinction between preparing for contingencies and being agile, as Guber and Buffett demonstrate, and having a Plan B. With a Plan B, you are not adjusting the route to your summit, you are changing your goal, and that's different. Studies have shown that people who have a Plan B are more likely to fail at Plan A. In one series of studies, Jihae Shin of the Wisconsin School of Business at the University of Wisconsin-Madison and Katherine Milkman of the Wharton School at the University of Pennsylvania asked hundreds of students to complete a task for free food and the opportunity to leave early. Some of the students were offered other opportunities to get the rewards even if they did not do well enough on the test. The researchers' other studies offered similar opportunities for rewards and, for some of the participants, opportunities to develop backup plans for earning those rewards. Without fail, those students with backup plans performed less well on the task. Debriefing the students at the end of the studies revealed that those with backup plans simply had less of a drive to complete the task.

Buffett never wavered from his goal of becoming very wealthy, very young. He just shifted the route to his success: it now went through New York City, and not Cambridge, Massachusetts.

When I failed to reach the summit of Everest, I never thought to myself, "Oh well, I'll substitute it for another summit." I doubt that any mountaineer ever reached a summit with the attitude, "If I don't make it, a different mountain will do." Instead, when I realized this attempt would not succeed, I told myself that I would try to reach the summit of Mt. Everest with a different but improved approach. My goal never changed, but I was flexible enough in my plans to accept the curve ball and react accordingly.

This reaction was part of my logistical plan in the sense that I was never going to recklessly endanger myself in a stubborn bid to achieve my goal. We will see in Chapter 6 what happens when mountain climbers become foolishly stubborn. Agility was baked into my goal, and that agility paid off.

IDENTIFY AND ACQUIRE THE RIGHT RESOURCES

An important goal of logistics is to make sure that you have the right resources to achieve the goal. Unfortunately, this is another reason that climbers die on Everest. They don't have the right resources in their pack. Rustem didn't even have the right clothes for the mountain. A one-piece summit suit was essential in the conditions that he was going to face to keep body heat in and wind out. For long-term pursuits that require persistence, the resources you have, including the tools to get the work done, can be just as essential as having the right tools on the mountain.

For example, I like to use a technology called Rocketbook. I can still physically write my notes, using a Frixion pen that can easily erase any of my notes. The tech also enables an easy scan from its app, and it automatically uploads to any email account, Google Drive, OneDrive, or dozens of other platforms for retaining my notes. This way, my daily summit is always in front of me. And if I have a call or a conversation or an idea, and I can't just take out my phone and jot it down, it's quick and easy for me to throw it right on the Rocketbook. Countless studies have shown the power of physically writing your words down. Whatever the tool that works for you, make sure it's one that can have your daily summit always present, and a place where you can easily write, achieve, and access anytime.

Also, it's my opinion the majority of your personal summits you are reaching for should be kept private. Some argue that you should share every goal with everyone to be held accountable, and while accountability is certainly a great boost for anything you're trying to achieve, I think personal goals are more attainable when you don't have the distraction of others quietly rooting against you. It's been said, and I agree, that the three things you keep private are your income, your love life, and *your next move*. Your goals are your next move. On my spiral-bound Rocketbook, I maintain a list on the left side for my professional to-dos and on the right side for my personal to-dos.

Remember that logistics is also about *efficiency*. For your long-term goal or quest, that means not just working hard but working smart, without wasting time and effort. There are a number of tools that help you progress toward your goal by clearing the barriers of unproductivity that will block your path.

One of these tools is called *Rescue Time*. Rescue Time is a time management tool—or more specifically, a time-wasting monitor. It's like having a stern, digital taskmaster looking over your shoulder and noting which programs and which websites you spend the most time on. It's also going to tell you which are your most productive and least productive work hours, weekdays and days of the month! You can even get filters that block out distracting sites. Apple and Android have built in apps to monitor screen time to let you know how much time you've squandered throughout the day!

One big problem for a lot of people is dealing with overflowing email in-boxes. There are several tools to help you with this problem. Sanebox creates a separate "SaneLater" in-box into which it funnels the emails that it has deduced are less important to you. Unroll.me is for all those email newsletters and other subscriptions that pile up in your in-box. It compiles all of these kinds of emails into one email bundle that you can check when you have time. It also gives you a complete list of all your subscriptions—and no doubt you'll be surprised by the number.

With some basic research, you will probably find the tool for all of those bad computer habits that are slowing you down and making you waste time.

And one of most egregious time wasters of our time is social media. According to a study by the marketing agency Mediakix, the average person will spend more than five years (five years and four months exactly) of their lives on social media. The five-year, four-months figure came from taking the average two hours a day that people spend on Youtube, Facebook, Snapchat, Instagram, Twitter, Tik Tok and (the next big time waster) and extrapolating those figures over a lifetime. For younger people, it's going to be a lot more than that, because according to Mediakix, it's not two hours a day that they spend on social media: it's *nine* hours a day. I thought that figure was unfathomable until we looked at my 16 year old daughter's average screen time: seven hours a day. Talk about parental fail!

Another problem with our growing addiction to social media is that we don't believe it's a problem. Smoking is an addiction, heavy drinking is an addiction, drugs are an addiction, but most people (59 percent, according to 2018 Pew Research statistics) believe they could give up all of social media if they wanted to. Even half of 18-24 year olds, according to the Pew survey, believe they can easily kick the social media addiction.

Don't get me wrong. Social media can be a powerful tool if it's used correctly. I'm on most social media platforms, and it's a fantastic way to present your material to those who need it. But I look at social media as a professional platform, not a way to escape work or life or that sparse minute that you're left to your own thoughts! For my personal social media time, I use a 90/10 rule. I spend 90% contributing, developing a post, and 10% consuming. Which is to say, I treat it like a polar plunge. Jump in, make a splash, and get out! If you're finding that too many trips down the rabbit hole of social media is undermining the persistent pursuit of your goal, use Rescue Time or Screen Time, or find the right productivity tool to set you right. Or remove social media all together.

HAVE A REALISTIC PICTURE OF HOW MUCH EFFORT YOU CAN EXPEND *AND* HOW MUCH TIME YOU NEED

I've put the last two lessons of logistics together because they are closely related. Failure can come from an unrealistic appraisal of the time and effort that you can put into a project or a goal. "I'll just do a couple of all-nighters and meet that deadline." "I'll just go to school by day and work nights to pay the bills."

Logistics is about *realistic* planning. It's about knowing the constraints of situations and of the people involved. Whatever your pursuit or your goal, you have to create a plan that is realistic and doable. Not easy—nothing worthwhile is easy. But doable.

Unfortunately, research shows that most of the time, we are not making reasonable, doable plans. This is known as the "planning fallacy," and it was first identified by Amos Tversky and Daniel Kahneman, two brilliant Israeli psychologists who also developed "prospect theory" (concerning decisions about risks, as well as the concept of fast and slow thinking). In their research, Kahneman and Tversky proved that, without fail, we systematically plan less time than needed for a task.

Later research by Canadian psychologist Roger Buehler tested and proved at least three reasons we consistently fall prey to the planning fallacy:

1) We underestimate our own completion times but not others'. In other words, we have a blind spot when it comes to our capabilities no matter how successful we are at planning the work of others.

2) We predict our time needs based on plan-based scenarios rather than relevant past experiences. Say, for example, that you want to write a paper or maybe you want to get a new job that will take you to the next level. In both cases, you might decide that you'll spend a month researching and writing the paper, or you might give yourself six months to find that job. You're deciding the scenario for the future, not paying attention to the fact that the last two papers you produced took several months each, and it took two years for you to find your current job—and you're aiming higher for the next one!

3) Even if we do remember past experiences, we just discount them. In his research, Buehler found that people always explain away past failures in time prediction, insisting that they are one-off experiences caused by exceptional circumstances. These people are wrong. So, if you know that you're going to underestimate the time needed to achieve something, what can you do about it? I incorporated extra weather days into our expeditions. This is where segmenting goals into sub-goals or milestones comes in, which I intuitively knew would be helpful, but which has also been proven by research. Two New Zealand researchers conducted a series of experiments to measure the impact of task segmentation on the

planning fallacy. What they found is that if you asked people to segment a task or project into a series of sub-tasks or sub-projects, the time they allocate for each of the sub-sections add up to more time than what they originally allocated to the entire project.

In other words, whatever goal you have—holding a balance posture in yoga, kicking your caffeine addiction, sailing to Hawaii—break that goal down into sub-goals. The time that you allocate for each of those sub-goals (building your yoga core, switching from coffee to tea, refining your tacking techniques) will be greater and more realistic than if you give yourself a general time frame.

As I close this chapter, we've come a long way from the tragedy of Rustem's death. On high-altitude mountains, paying attention to details can be a matter of life and death. For most of our pursuits and goals, the stakes are not as high. But as Henry David Thoreau said, most men live lives of quiet desperation. And, said Oliver Wendell Holmes, die with their music still in them. But ultimately, if you want to reach the summit of your dreams, you also need to pay attention to the details. Even the detail as seemingly benign but immensely impactful of what to listen to when you have nothing to hear. Your decision could help make the difference between successfully breaking through and reaching your summit, or spending your time seething in frustration as your goal remains out of reach.

CHAPTER FIVE

IT STARTS FROM THE OUTSIDE IN: PREPARING YOUR BODY FOR PERSISTENCE

To keep the body in good health is a duty...otherwise we shall not be able to keep our mind strong and clear.

– Buddha

This meat suit that's transporting you through this journey in life is the only one you've got, and it can take a lot. It's meant to work really hard. It can be abused, neglected, and, put through every conceivable deprivation and still be the most efficient and effective living organism on the planet. And without a doubt, the strength of our body is connected to how long and strong we can persist in physical and mental tasks.

PERSISTENCE IS PHYSICAL

Obviously, climbing mountains is an intense physical endeavor. But don't be fooled. No matter what your goal, without exception, you need to have your best physical frame if you want to succeed. And as we've learned from coach Karl Turk and comedian Lee Ridley, physical disability has less to do the with the frame you have been given, and more about what you make of it.

Because *persistence is physical.* Persistence requires a focused and continued effort, and *any* effort will take a toll on your mind and body. We often link physical effort to physical goals only. We admire the young Olympic swimmer who takes the cold plunge into the pool every morning at 4 a.m. before school. We recognize the physical training of our favorite athletes. We appreciate the physical endurance of mixed martial artists.

But we don't think of the medical resident's 15-hour days in her quest to become a surgeon as a physical achievement. We don't think of the entrepreneur who works deep into the night every night tinkering with his vacuum that eventually takes the world by storm as a physical achievement. We don't think of the adult student getting up at 5 a.m. to work on her master's before going to the office as a physical achievement. The fact is that every persistent worthwhile effort, whether it's physical or mental, whether it's short-term or long-term, requires you to be in good physical shape.

LOSING MY BREATH

It doesn't take long to recognize that high-altitude climbing is truly breathtaking. And I don't mean that in the "it's so breathtakingly beautiful I could almost cry" sense (although it's that, too). I mean that high-altitude climbing literally takes your breath away.

Controlled breathing quickly became evident and critically important as my pursuit of the world's highest peaks took me into higher and thinner air. Early on in my climbing career, we set out to summit the highest peak in Central America and third highest peak in North America—a dormant stratovolcano named Pico de Orizaba. Located 145 miles east of Mexico City, the peak rises to an impressive 18,491 feet. A mixed rock-and-ice climb, Pico De Orizaba is widely viewed as an excellent training mountain for those who desire to transition from hiking peaks to climbing mountains. It has just the right amount of technical climbing that, while challenging, is not overwhelming for nascent mountaineers. Additionally, the ability to stage from the stone hut (Piedra Grande) at 14,000 feet allows climbers to quickly experience high altitude climbing without exhausting themselves on the climb to higher camps. Piedra Grande is accessible from the charming city of Tlachichuca—after a bone-rattling four-hour drive on a winding track up the stunning Mexican countryside. It's one of the few peaks where you can drive your gear and stage at 14,000 feet.

Our summit attempt began with an alpine start, which allowed us to reach and climb the glacier while the surface was still frozen. Interestingly, on steeper pitches, it is safer at times and easier to traverse when the ground is still icy, allowing your crampons to firmly bite. We reached the foot of the Jamapa glacier, a 50-degree slope, around 4:00 a.m. At 17,000 feet—a new altitude record for me—the glacier stretched in front of us and led directly to the volcano's summit rim.

I stopped to catch my breath *and quickly realized there was nothing to catch*. I inhaled deeply, and while the volume of air filling my lungs was there, the oxygen wasn't. It was a disquieting experience. Hesitantly, I inhaled again and got a similar result. I also had the distinct impression of a detectible drop in energy as well. What was happening to me? For the first time in the mountains, I noticed the measurable effect of breathing at altitude. After orienting myself to this new realization, I was able to continue up the mountain, but was forced to inhale twice the volume of air to deliver the same amount of oxygen to my bloodstream. The concentration of oxygen in the air was the same, but in the thin air, the density of those molecules is dispersed, and you need to suck in more air to capture the same amount of oxygen.

Any mountaineer who desires to be successful in high altitudes quickly understands that it's imperative to study, practice, and apply specific breathing techniques that are designed to maximize oxygen uptake efficiently. Taking a breath is the first and last thing each of us will ever do in this life. How effective you are with the 700 million breaths you take in and out on this planet (give or take a few million) will have a direct effect on nearly every aspect of your life. We take our breaths for granted, or rather we don't even have to think about it, because breathing is part of our autonomic nervous system—that wonderful selfless action of our body that proceeds without our conscious direction, just like our heartbeat and digestive processes.

In certain situations, however, we have to override and take control of our body's automatic processes to produce a more controlled and, ideally, better result. This would be similar to my climbing partner, Tom (an airline captain), taking his plane's control off automatic pilot.

It turns out that our greatest physical tool for taking control of our bodies is none other than what you're doing right now: breathing. Science has proven that managing our breathing allows us to take control of our physical state and our mental state, even allowing us to voluntarily venture into parts of our brain that we previously thought were inaccessible.

Mountaineers use breathing as a technique to help combat the effects of the thin atmosphere once they are climbing the mountain. The technique combines belly breathing—expanding your abdomen as you take in a breath to store the greatest amount of air possible—with a forced exhale, which means blowing out through pursed lips as much air as possible as strongly as possible. For many people, the only time they force exhale is when they blow out their birthday candles—or perhaps, when they take a breathalyzer test. This combination of belly breathing and forced exhale is what we call *pressure breathing*, and increases the pressure in your lungs—a vital counter-response to the decreased atmospheric pressure of high altitudes. Pressure breathing, however, makes the muscles in your lungs work very hard; so here's another part of the training that mountaineers go through before they get on the mountain: working those lung muscles so they will be able to pressure breathe when they start reaching the higher altitudes.

Taking control of your breathing is not just for the mountains. In fact, you already use controlled breathing, probably more than you realize. For example, if you are extremely tense and want to calm down, what do you do? *Take a deep breath.* When you take that deep breath, you've taken your breathing off of automatic pilot.

And there's much more than you can do with controlled breathing. When I want to change my state, whether it's a physical funk or an emotional rut, I take a deep inhale and a forceful pursed-lips exhale. As a bonus, I'll at times throw my hands forward like I'm throwing a Street Fighter II Ryu fireball to engage my physiology. Try it, it'll snap you out of whatever state you don't want to be in quicker than just about anything else—and all it takes is one breath.

Breathing is also how we rid our body of fat, according to physicist Ruben Meerman. Meerman says that as we try to lose weight, we don't think about *where* that weight that we're carrying around right now will go. Some might think that fat leaves our bodies through our sweat, or through our "poop" (to use Meerman's technical term). Meerman explains that the chemical equation for fat is $C_{55}H_{104}O_6$, with C standing for Carbon, H for Hydrogen, and O for oxygen. He then explains that fat with oxygen will turn into carbon dioxide and water (the chemical equation if you're interested is $C_{55}H_{104}O_6 + 78O_2 \rightarrow 55CO_2 + 52H_2O$). Since you inhale oxygen by breathing, and you exhale carbon dioxide by, you guessed it, breathing, the core mechanism for getting rid of your fat is breathing! Meerman did say fat turns into carbon dioxide *and water*, and that's true, but based on Meerman's mathematics, the water part is pretty low. For every 10 kg of fat that we lose, 8.5 kg comes out as carbon dioxide, 1.6 kg comes out as water H2O (sweat, tears, urine etc.). Bottom line: exercise is a great way to remove fat because it makes us sweat—but even more, it makes us breathe harder!

YOUR HEART IN THE MOUNTAINS

Understanding how altitude impacts our physiology not only helps us anticipate what can happen at altitude, but can also be applied to the thicker air at normal altitudes. It's a little-known fact that the heart needs the same amount of oxygen to complete a push up on a sandy beach as it does standing on the top of a Himalayan peak. The problem is that at the summit of Mount Everest, our body can only intake 20 percent of the oxygen it can intake at sea level. In my experience, at an altitude as significant as the slopes of Everest, it takes three, four, or *five* times the exertion to get the same level of oxygen into my body that I can get with one inhaled breath at sea level. This explains why at the summit of Everest, climbers are 80 percent slower at everything they do, whether it's setting up a tent, putting on your boots, or trying to figure out a simple math problem (because lack of oxygen is not just a physical problem, it also affects your mental abilities). There is a limitation on the volume of air our lungs hold—a capacity of about eight liters per minute. Above 26,000 feet, commonly referred to as the Death Zone, the air you can draw in and out reaches our lungs' limit quickly. This means that the amount of blood that gets pumped through your body with each heartbeat is significantly reduced.

So how does the body react when each heartbeat is less productive? Simple: if each heartbeat is not pumping enough oxygen through our system, then our heart beats faster. If at the top of Everest, it takes five heartbeats to pump the oxygen that one beat pumps at sea level, then our body is going to try to get those five heartbeats done as quickly as possible.

Physically, here's how it works: Once your body recognizes it's now into thin air, it automatically kicks your diaphragm into overdrive, increasing your respiratory rate, which increases your heart rate, which in turn results in bone marrow producing new red blood cells faster.

In training for climbs, I base my aerobic workouts mostly on a desired target heart rate. I train within the desired zones so I know how fast or long I can move, and I also focus on the correct target heart rate to increase mitochondria production. My resting heart rate before I left home for Everest was 48 beats per minute. Resting at Everest base camp, at 17,000 feet it was 68, at Camp 1 at 19,600 feet it was 105, and when trying my best to rest before the summit push at Camp 4 at 26,000 feet, I put my finger on my neck and counted a pulse of 120 beats per minute. I would have thought that a higher heart rate for an in-shape climber would be no problem, but in fact, your maximum heart rate decreases the higher the altitude: your heart's stroke volume drops which increases the exertion required of your heart to deliver oxygen to the starved muscles.

THE PHYSICALITY OF DAY-TO-DAY PERSISTENCE

Perhaps one of the greatest physical challenges of persistence is managing our day-to-day energy. Succeeding in the long run by dealing on a daily basis with the hurdles and pitfalls that life throws at you requires unflagging energy. And the time we take to create or destroy our energy is up to us. Because the only thing truly equal in life is the amount of time each person is given in a day. We weren't born equal, we don't have the same opportunities, and advantages and disadvantages are not spread equally across different people. What is fair is that you and I can control what we do during our 16-20 waking hours each day.

There are many books and blogs about mastering your morning. Starting the day off right can set you up for success. But the right morning starts 5-8 hours before you wake up. Dialing in your proper sleep is becoming more and more important as we learn the mental and physical cleansing effects of sleep. Proper room temperature, light, pillows, daily reflection, and limiting caffeine and alcohol at least 3 hours before rest all contribute to that effective morning laying ahead.

I've never needed an alarm. That's something that my wife can't comprehend. When I'm not on the road, I work from home. I have a home gym where I work out based upon objectives, which is usually a mountain. I have two numbers written on the mirror: the altitude of the summit of the peak I'm training for and the altitude of my home: 4,280 feet. The second is a continual reminder that no matter how far we climb to that first number, the second is where I must return. For my workout cool down, I have an app that guides my meditation for seven minutes. The meditation varies depending on what suits the day: Finding Your Focus to Tame Your Anxiety, Slay Your Stress to Find Your Calm. Seven minutes or less is what works for me, and there are several popular meditation apps and hundreds of guided meditations that can work for you.

I take a shower and, at the end, turn my back and crack it to cold. Harvard professor David Sinclair says we need cold exposure.

According to Sinclair, cold exposure builds up brown fat that has a lot of mitochondria and secretes little proteins to tell the body to be healthy. Sinclair further states that in our society today, we're always warm. He has something called the Metabolic Winter Hypothesis. Because we wear a jacket to go from our car to the restaurant, sleep with the covers on, or turn up the heat at any sign of chill, we never get exposed to cold unless we force ourselves. But if we give ourselves a bit of chill, we turn on our brown fat, increase our metabolism, and build mitochondria—which is exactly what mountaineers train to do before we head to the hill.

I do calf raises for the two minutes of my time on my electric toothbrush. As I continue to get ready in the morning, I listen to a Ted talk on my Alexa device or some form of informative video on YouTube from a thought leader—anything that will carry me through the morning. I also try to drink a 6 oz. glass of water. I take a supplement specifically designed based on the blood work that I have done and my specific needs. I try to have some form of protein in an egg. All of this really sets me up to battle the day ahead.

THERE'S NO ESCALATOR TO THE TOP

Staying physically fit requires dedication. So many people talk about losing weight or running regularly, but most simply don't have the dedication to make it happen. Dedication trumps motivation. Motivation is battling for fitness equipment the first morning on a cruise. Dedication is having your pick at the empty gym on Friday. There's one common trait through all the sports

Hall of Fame halls: Dedication. The persistent quality to continue and repeat the winning process year after year.

My friend KC made it a goal to run at least a mile every day for a full year. When his anticipated run that evening was interrupted by his flight delay, KC ran one mile up and down the terminal at Philadelphia airport. His dedication has led to finishing the Boston Marathon and running several 100-mile mountain races.

When my friend Brooke made a goal to add one squat each day starting at the New Year, nothing stopped her. She did this every day. When we were vacationing on a houseboat in Lake Powell, Utah, even after leg-burning sessions of wake surfing all day, there was Brooke at 11:00 p.m. squatting on September 5th (248 squats). When we were in a RV vacationing with our families for fall break from school, Brooke was in the cramped hallway busting out squat number 291 (October 18th). Throughout the whole year, she only missed the two days when her slipped rib made it unbearable to breathe, let alone stand up. In any environment, she found a way. No excuses. And by December 31, 2019, she had squatted 66,985 times.

After summiting Everest, my friend Dan said "no thanks" to the celebratory cake passed around at base camp, holding true to his 18-year no dessert policy— he had his cake but did not eat it too. Dedication trumps motivation. What persistence starts, dedication finishes.

In my own way, I try to show similar dedication to keeping fit. For example, one of the best ways to keep fit is simply to take the stairs. It's almost become a joke now with my wife as we approach a set of airport escalators with a staircase in between them. With a quick sly glance, she has always taken the escalator, I've taken the stairs. Recently, she has begun joining me on the staircase, even sometimes trying to race me to the top, proving that sometimes a little healthy competition can help people to reach a little higher. As Jesús Peteiro, MD, PhD, a cardiologist at University Hospital A Coruña in Spain explained in an article on Health.com, *"If you can walk up four floors without stopping, you have good functional capacity. If not, it's a good indication that you need more exercise."*

Because I'm on the road a lot for work, I have limited control replicating my mountaineering training. There are not a whole lot of stair climbers in the fitness rooms at the Holiday Inn Express. So during my Everest training, I packed a 30-liter small day bag with a 20-liter dry bag—those bags used for river rafting to keep your gear dry. A dry bag is used to keep water out, but in my case, I put 30 pounds of water in, and use it as a weighted back for climbing stairs. I try to book my hotel stays around which hotel is the tallest.

I once had an early morning flight out of Seattle and my hotel for the night was the Crown Plaza, as its 12-story emergency fire stairs made a perfect silo for my workout. With my audio book set and my dry bag full, I began the up and down climbing of the steps. About 10 minutes in, my intestinal battle with a Chipotle burrito from the previous night began.

And I was losing. I had two choices: bail out and head back to the room or exert all the willpower and force in my existence and continue. I figured there might be a no-stop-to-drop scenario on a summit day, and so I kept climbing and slowly descending the 12 flights up and down—for sixty minutes.

In many ways, a staircase makes a good analogy for the persistence required for success. Or, to put it another way, there is no escalator to the top. Get used to taking the stairs.

PUT YOUR SHOULDERS BACK

I'm going to close this chapter with something completely different but amazingly important.

I was, and still am, a lanky pile of limbs. Growing up, the common phrase repeated to me by my well-meaning mother was, "David, put your shoulders back!" While hunched over the TV watching Mr. Belvedere after school, I'd hear from the kitchen, "put your shoulders back!" Same thing when slumped over playing Super Mario Bros or at the dining table: "Put your shoulders back!" I started correcting myself and have found that my mom may have had more inspiration than just trying to correct a slouch. *Your outside demeanor and posture greatly reflect your inner disposition.*

It's surprisingly easy to recognize someone's current disposition simply by observing their posture and how they are carrying themselves, if you pay attention. Even when we aren't consciously observing people's demeanor, we intuitively "read" what their body is presenting and react accordingly.

We had just arrived into Camp 2 (21,000 feet) on Everest for our summit push and entered the communal dining tent where a "United Nations" of climbers sought solace and restoration. On this day, the climbing season's first victors and casualties of the various summit attempts came stumbling into camp. While I was enjoying some hot lemon tea, two climbers from Spain achingly shuffled into the tent. They both sat down with a force, as if they had unloaded the mountain itself when doing so. When you arrive into Camp 2 after a summit attempt, you have been climbing for 36 straight hours. Their shoulders caved, haunted expressions etching their faces, eyes staring unseeingly, which revealed the answer to whether they had summited or not. Quickly, the kitchen Sherpas brought them some garlic soup, and they soon warmed to some semblance of life. I never ask a fellow climber if they had summited, although in this instance I already knew. I did ask, sincerely, "How was your attempt?" One of the Spaniard climbers looked across at me and said, "We came within 200 meters of the summit until the frostbite was too much." The enormity of his situation—the summit being only 660 feet from where he turned, the condition of his bulbous fingertips indicative of frostbite, and his obvious anguish, humbled me to my core. Then he began to weep. And I wept with him. I told him that while "I don't understand how *you* feel, on our previous attempt we came within 100 meters of the summit before turning." He outstretched his frostbitten hands to take mine and said, "Then, you do understand."

While the posture of the Spaniards radiated defeat and foretold their story, the next climbers through the tent door were a Russian group who had reached the summit, in this same storm and weather as the Spaniards. The goggles of one of the Russians had frosted over early in the climb, so he had climbed the better part of the summit day without eye protection. He shuffled into the dining tent with the aid of his Sherpa and gently sat down, sporting a pair of sunglasses under a new pair of goggles to omit any light from entering his eye slits. Totally snow blind, he had a smile on his face. A physician from Seattle was placing the Spaniards' frozen toes into a pot of warm water when she moved on to assist the Russian's snow blindness. She mixed a cocktail of saline and lidocaine, and every 15 minutes she would remove his sunglasses and goggles to perform the torturous routine of prying his eyes open and administering the liquid relief. The Russian was upright, alert, and chatting, apparently unaffected by the sensation of sandpaper scratching his corneas that accompanies snow blindness.

Both climbers, the Spaniard and the Russian, were in extreme pain, but one had the additional burden of mental anguish, while the other had the elation of achieving what he had so strongly desired. We all carry pain, but our degree of suffering can be increased or decreased by how we choose to carry it upon our shoulders. I certainly didn't expect the Spaniard to be joyous with frostbite and a failed summit. Nor the Russian to be sullen, even with temporary blindness, after standing atop of the world. But I learned an important lesson: how you hold yourself declares how you feel inside. And that means that *changing* the way you hold yourself can, to a large degree, *change* the way you feel.

Even if you didn't have an attentive mother correcting your posture, or you have been beaten down by bullies or abuse, you can always immediately alter your disposition by altering your posture.

If you shuffle around with the posture of a defeated person, others will naturally assign you a lower status, and this will translate to a lower status within your own psychosis and lower your own serotonin. As a result, you may retreat from taking that next step up when you could've climbed higher. It can affect every area of life. You could refuse to throw your name into the hat for that promotion, you could limit your network opportunities or cut off a chance with a desirable partner before it even begins. You might end up feeling like a victim whose only salvation can be found at the bottom of some form of bottle. Eventually, physical ailments may follow.

On the other side, rolling your shoulders back, you will feel more ready to deal with whatever the world presses down upon you. Simple alterations have profound effects. One day in second grade, I fell ill and told my teacher. She sent me down to the school nurse. The nurse was busy with someone else's runny nose, so as I sat in the resting room, there stapled to the carpeted wall were large cut out letters that read: "Smile, you'll feel better." I did, and I did! Emotion is partly bodily expression and can be amplified or dampened by that expression.

It's not only how *you* feel, but also how *others* think of you. If you slump down, and you *look* small and defeated, then you will in effect *feel* small and defeated. And others around you will size you up as small and defeated. The sociologist Charles Cooley said, "I am not who you think I am; I am not who I think I am; I am who I think you think I am."

So, as part of your preparation to be persistent, even something like changing your posture can make a difference, because it will make you feel stronger.

"Power poses," a concept developed by former Harvard Business School professor Amy Cuddy, is perhaps the most famous example of how deliberately working on your posture and body language can change how strong and powerful you feel. Basing her theory on the results of her 2010 academic study, which after some academic controversy was backed by further research published in 2018, Cuddy argues that adopting an expansive pose—that is an open pose with arms and legs away from the body—will make a person feel more powerful and as a result, act more confidently. There are a number of different power poses, perhaps the most famous being the Wonder Woman pose, in which you stand feet apart, hands on your hips and you chin tilted slightly upward. The Wonder Woman pose is the opposite of the slouching, head down, hands tucked close to the body posture of those who feel powerless. Cuddy suggests adopting and holding the power pose for a few minutes before entering the arena in which you need to be self-confident, such as a job interview or a presentation.

In her book, *Presence*, Cuddy explains that power poses work because the body has a "primitive" and direct connection to the mind. If your body reflects confidence, it tells your mind that you *are* confident. In a way, power poses are similar to the deep breath that a performer might take before coming on stage or the shoulder-punching pep talks that athletes engage in before running onto the fields. You are no longer intellectually preparing yourself, but letting the primitive, physical you take over your mind.

Cuddy became famous through her 2012 TedX talk, which has been viewed over 56 million times. But long before there were laptops to ruin your posture and Ted Talks or YouTube exercise videos to fix it, my mom was vigilant in keeping my posture correct. I know it wasn't just about aesthetics. She instinctively knew that how you hold yourself impacts how you feel and, just as important to my mom, how others look at you.

Persistence is physical. Don't be fooled into thinking that physical preparation is for athletes and people focused on their looks; your physical preparation will help you overcome the hardships and setbacks that can defeat a weaker person.

Persistence rests on the twin pillars of mental and physical strength—strength in the sense of a healthy body. A healthy body is one that has the stamina and core strength to make it through long days and to combat the mental stress of setbacks and challenges. No matter where we are or what we're doing, we all can manage our breath and our posture anytime to put you in a peak state.

PART THREE

SUSTAINING PERSISTENCE

CHAPTER SIX

THE DARK SIDE OF
PERSISTENCE

I learn from everybody even if it's what not to do.

- Abraham Lincoln

Persistence is at the heart of achievement and success in nearly every endeavor. Mountain climbing offers one of the most vivid examples of why, without persistence, you will probably fail.

Unfortunately, mountain climbing reveals just as vividly the *dark side* of persistence. When pushed too far, when pushed beyond the limits of reason, persistence becomes a liability, not an asset. It sets the stage for failure, not success.

We begin, as always, in the mountains, where foolish persistence can have tragic consequences. The majority of client deaths that occur on Mt. Everest are not the result of accidents or harsh conditions, but instead begin with a single act, or worse, repeated acts, of obstinacy—climbers who refuse to stop and turn around, who keep going, who, as someone once said, "keep walking until they die."

SHRIYA SHAH-KLORFINE SUMMITS EVEREST...

One morning, I was working out and watching an Everest climbing documentary about a Nepalese-born Canadian named Shriya Shah-Klorfine. Halfway through the documentary, I saw a familiar face on the screen: Temba Sherpa, who was my lead Sherpa on my Everest expedition. I can't say enough about the professionalism and competence of Temba Sherpa. On our climb, he was a steady calm supporter of our climbing team. As he described to the TV cameras how he kept pushing Klorfine down the mountain, repeating to her in Nepalese, "Walk, sister, walk, sister, please walk, Shriya sister," I can still hear Temba's words of assurance to me as we continued up and down each perilous section of the Khumbu Icefall or the Lhotse Face: "Keep each step simple and firm. Keep each step simple and firm."

The harrowing climb of Shriya Shah-Klorfine, described in detail in the documentary, must be one of the toughest memories of Temba's career—especially since both the owner of the expedition company and Shriya's lead Sherpa would eventually leave her behind, putting all the pressure on Temba and one other Sherpa to guide the all too common inexperienced mountain climbers that continue to attempt Everest.

The story of Shriya Klorfine is a case study in the dark side of persistence.

Shriya was born in Nepal in the shadow of Mt. Everest. As a child, she looked at the mountain and vowed that some day she would climb. For a while, that dream was forgotten as she left

Nepal to explore the world. Eventually, she married Canadian Bruce Klorfine and moved to Toronto, Canada. In Toronto, she started a business importing Indian food and spices. She also dabbled in politics. And then, in 2011, at the age 33 and without any mountain climbing experience whatsoever, Shriya announced to her family and friends that she was going to climb Mt. Everest.

Friends and family, including her husband, tried desperately to talk her out of it, but she was stubborn and refused to change her mind. Instead, Shriya began "training" for Everest by taking long hikes in the Ontario countryside. She also practiced climbing … on an indoor rock wall. I can tell you that neither leisurely hikes in the country nor climbing a rock wall are going to help you in any way to climb Mt. Everest.

Eventually, Shriya returned to her native Nepal and continued her training by taking long hikes around Kathmandu. The one thing she had going for her was that, unlike many climbers, the altitude did not cause her problems—she did not endure the nausea or fatigue that many climbers must overcome. However, according to the documentary, she was extremely slow and had to be taught everything about mountain climbing—even how to put on crampons (and how to use them).

Somehow, however, despite being perhaps the slowest of the hundreds of climbers on Mt. Everest that day, Shriya made it as far as Camp 4. But that's when the lead Sherpa of the expedition, horrified by the slow pace of Shriya and her lack of fitness, refused to lead her any further. A cousin describes in the documentary how Shriya called her family and described what the lead Sherpa had told her: "If you go on and walk this way, you will die, and you will kill us, too."

At this point, the lead Sherpa made the decision to abandon her at Camp 4, leaving Temba to deal with this daunting situation alone. A ridiculously inexperienced climber, and the owner of his company and the lead Sherpa bailing. And, as it turns out, one of the worst seasons in Everest history. The legendary expedition leader Russell Brice had, in fact, cancelled his expeditions outright that year (May 2012), telling dozens of his clients that there would be no attempt this year (and no refund of the $50,000 fee) because the Khumbu icefall was unstable. Two years later, in 2014, the section that Russell Brice was concerned about gave way and killed 16 Sherpas in what was the deadliest day on Everest at the time.

Despite all of these reasons for turning back, Shriya persisted in her summit attempt, and somehow, at 11:30 a.m. on May 19th, after 16 straight hours of climbing, Shriya, Temba and her second Sherpa reached the final obstacle before the summit, the Hillary Step. This was a 40-foot wall of rock and ice with a single rope line for the climbers going up *and* the climbers going down.

Having successfully summited and heading down the mountain, the expedition company owner and the lead Sherpa crossed Shriya as she was waiting to go up the Hillary Step. With only 20 minutes of oxygen left, they told her that it was impossible for her to successfully summit. Once again, she was told that she was going to die if she continued. And once again, she ignored the warnings. Instead, she told them, "I've spent the money, and my goal is to reach the summit." So the expedition company owner gave her one last bottle of oxygen, then continued down the mountain.

So Shriya and the two Sherpas with her, including my friend Temba, continued, getting through the Hillary Step and, just before 2:30 p.m. on May 19, 2012, finally reaching the summit.

It took her 20 hours to reach the summit from Camp 4. And the oxygen that she had received at the Hillary Step 11 hours earlier would have lasted her 4 hours. She had done all her climbing through what is known as the Death Zone without oxygen. Still, elated by reaching the summit, Shriya spent 30 minutes savoring the moment—30 minutes she did not have.

Finally, just before 3 p.m., Shriya and the Sherpas started their descent. There were only a few hours of daylight left, the wind was steadily increasing to hurricane force, and the temperatures had started to plunge to minus 40 degrees. Shriya, barely moving, was urged forward by Temba and the other Sherpa, with continued entreaties to "walk, sister." They used the common Nepalese word *didi*: "Walk, didi, walk, didi." For seven hours they stumbled slowly down. When climbers passed her on the way up, she would plead with them, "Please help me, please don't let me die." Temba later told me he continued to urge her forward. When they reached the area known as "the Balcony," Shriya stopped moving and stopped talking. After trying all they could do to get her to move or show some sign of life, there was nothing more for Temba and the other Sherpa to do. They secured her to the rope line and left her there.

For ten days, Shriya's frozen corpse stayed on the 27,500-foot Balcony until a recovery party brought the body down. Shriya Shah-Klorfine would be cremated in her hometown of Kathmandu.

Throughout the entire experience, multiple people—from her husband and friends when she first told them her plans to the various Sherpas and guides who warned her explicitly that she would die—tried to change Shriya Shah-Klorfine's mind. But she persisted. As Everest journalist Grayson Schaeffer, a writer and editor for *Outside* magazine, explains in the documentary, "Every year, there will be a slow blood-letting of people who probably shouldn't be there, go anyway, who don't listen to reason, and who end up walking until they die."

FROM PERSISTENCE TO OBSESSION

The dark side of persistence takes many forms. As we'll see later in this chapter, too much persistence in sales translates into *aggressiveness*. In leadership, too much persistence is reflective in the *inflexibility* of the leader or the company that refuses to change or to let go of the past.

One of the darkest sides of persistence, however, is *obsession*. Obsession is built on the foundation of persistence, of refusing to accept limits, or to accept moderation, or to accept defeat.

NO SURRENDER

Maybe one of the strangest tales of the dark side of persistence is the story of World War II Japanese Army soldier Hiroo Onoda.

Onoda was an intelligence officer sent to Lubang in 1944 to lead covert operations to halt the American advance across the Pacific. One of his goals was to destroy the island's pier and runway to prevent an American invasion of the island. His superiors refused to allow the destruction. In February 1945, the American troops landed and took over the island. Onoda and three members of his unit escaped into the jungle.

In August of 1945, Japan surrendered, and the war was over. Onoda and his companions noticed that military operations on the island decreased significantly, *but they refused to believe that the war was over.* His companions were soon captured or killed by Filipino authorities, but Onoda remained at large, convinced that the war was continuing. Even when leaflets were dropped from the island with photos and messages from his family, Onoda refused to believe what he was reading. "I assumed they were living under the occupation and had to obey the authorities to survive," he said later.

Onoda persisted in believing that the war still raged on ... for nearly 30 years! During that time, he hid in the jungles of the Filipino island of Lubang, subsisting on rice, coconuts, and meat from stolen cattle, and eluding the Filipino soldiers sent after him.

In a bizarre twist, Onoda was finally located not by Filipino police who had been chasing him for years, but by Norio Suzuki, a Japanese student and aspiring explorer. In early 1974, Suzuki came upon Onoda after just four days of searching, and according to reports, impressed Onoda with his calm demeanor as the old soldier trained his gun on him. "Onoda-san, the Emperor and the people of Japan are worried about you," the young man said. Still,

Onoda refused to surrender until he had a direct order from his commanding officer, Major Yoshimi Taniguchi. A month later, his commanding officer, who was thankfully still alive and now a bookseller, traveled to Lubang and assured Onoda that the Imperial command had ceased all activity and that he could thus honorably lay down his arms. On March 11, 1974, Onoda surrendered, and for the first time in 29 years, left the jungle of Lubang. He would be pardoned by then-Philippines President Ferdinand Marcos and allowed to return to Japan.

Back in his home country, Onoda wrote a bestseller called, *No Surrender: My Thirty Year War.* Unable to cope with crowded, modern Japan, he moved to Brazil, where he became a cattle farmer. In a 2001 interview, Onoda explained his persistence in fighting the war decades after its end. "On Lubang, I didn't want to be seen as a failure," he said. "So I protected my honor and carried out my mission to the end." Onoda died in January 2014, at the age of 91. As he told a journalist after his surrender, "I was defiant and stubborn in everything I did. I was born like that. That was my fate."

BALANCING ACT: AVOIDING TOO MUCH PERSISTENCE IN SALES AND LEADERSHIP

In business and professional careers, the dark side of persistence does not have the tragic consequences of obsession on the mountain. Still, the same "tipping point" effect occurs: what is at first the key to success becomes a path to failure.

For example, sales, as with mountain climbing, is not for the faint of heart. You will never be a successful salesperson if you do not have a healthy, even exceptional, measure of persistence within your character. But as with mountaineers, the very fact that persistence is so essential to success is the reason that salespeople often exemplify the dark side of persistence—not knowing when to accept a "no" and even mistreating any prospect who dares to hesitate in response to his or her sales pitch.

I've been in sales my whole life. I spent my 20's in the wireless telecom space, then pivoted to public sector software sales in my 30's, all the while building our international adventure travel businesses. I've never once had the certainty of the same amount on my monthly paychecks, and for me, that's okay. I like having the ability to grow territories, represent products, or win or lose business based upon my direct efforts.

My former counterpart in software sales for the eastern U.S. took a much different approach. With a failing quota looming, he pushed his prospects and eventually pushed himself out of the position. One of his final deals had the prospect calling his manager saying, "We refuse to work with him."

In her article, "8 Tips for Dealing with Pushy Salespeople," author Suzanne Raga differentiates between the "assertive" salesperson—the type of salesperson I would say has the required persistence to succeed—and the "aggressive" salesperson. Here's how she describes the difference: "If you're waffling on whether to make a purchase, an assertive salesperson may provide more information or respectfully ask you what he can do to help you make your decision. An aggressive salesperson, on the other hand, may threaten to revoke a discounted price, complain that your indecision is wasting his time, or refuse to accept that you don't want to make a purchase."

Aggressive salespeople will also put pressure on a prospect with an artificial deadline, manipulating you into thinking that it's now or never. I agree with Raga: If a salesperson tells you that you must buy an item now, and says that you're not allowed to take time to think about it or do more research, consider that a red flag.

According to Peter Caputa, longtime VP of Sales at marketing software developer Hubspot, too much persistence is the opposite of what successful sales is supposed to be about: helping people with their needs: "Don't let the pursuit of your personal goals lead you to conclude that aggressiveness is necessary—especially to the point where it costs you the trust of your prospects. Your goals and your commitment to helping should never be in opposition."

Salespeople will stay on the productive side of persistence if they understand that there's a balance between too little and too much persistence, Caputa writes. "If you've received a cease-and-desist letter, you've probably gone too far," he writes. "However, if you're living on Twitter all day waiting for that perfect conversation-starter to pop up in your feed, you're probably letting your fear of rejection prevent you from doing what you need to do."

Ironically, I have found what Hubspot Asia Senior Marketing Manager Niti Shah describes in the article as pulling back—what she calls "breaking up"—can often spark the response they had been pursuing from the beginning. According to Shah, "You're letting the prospect know that you've tried to get in touch with them, and that since this might not be the best time to connect for them, you don't want to bother them if there's no fit. In other words, use the break-up email as a way to remind the prospect one last time that you've been trying to get in touch. Ironically, this is the email that gets the highest response rate for many of the salespeople I spoke to when researching this post."

The same balance—knowing when persistence has turned into a liability and not an asset, also happens in leadership. Just as with sales, successful leadership requires persistence … up to a point. In the arena of leadership, too much persistence becomes inflexibility. As Dan Rockwell, author of the popular Leadership Freak blog, quips, "Persistent problems indicate too much persistence. The dark side of persistence is inflexibility, stubbornness, resistance, hardheadedness, and a closed mind. *When persistence is unwillingness to adapt, you're doomed.*" [his italics]

There are three principle reasons leaders become what he calls "hardheaded," according to Rockwell:

1) History. It worked in the past.

2) Attachment. They fall in love with their ideas.

3) Ego. Adapting feels like failure.

The best leaders, Rockwell writes, stop doing what is not working. "Stopping is one of leadership's greatest challenges." One of the most iconic stories of misguided persistence in business history is the demise of Kodak. As digital photography emerged,

Kodak stayed welded to film—even though digital photography was being developed in Kodak's own R&D labs! Kodak's persistence led this once great company to bankruptcy.

Kodak's story is not unique. Business history is filled with once-powerful companies taken down by new companies with new ideas. The "incumbent" companies, as they are known, have an overwhelming advantage, including massive resources and a captive customer base, to defeat any upstarts; their mistake, however, is to persist in what they've done in the past, leaving the door open to the newcomers. IBM persisted in focusing on mainframes and mini-computers, ignoring the personal computer revolution until late in the game and thus squandering what could have been an insurmountable advantage. IBM would cede the advantage again by persisting with its DOS operating system, allowing Apple to be the first to offer the customer friendly and intuitive graphic user interface. (While Steve Jobs did not steal the graphic user interface concept from Xerox Parc—it was part of an agreement—it's obvious Jobs realized better than Xerox Parc the potential of the new technology.) Apple would benefit once again when market-dominating Blackberry failed to appreciate the danger of Apple's iPhone.

The case of Blackberry is a typical business lesson of the dark side of persistence. I was working the wireless telecom sector during the heyday of Blackberry. I was in charge of selling all types of mobile handsets to all mobile carriers. I loved my Blackberry and held on to its hardware as long as possible, but they didn't adapt, and my roller ball Blackberry was discarded for a new touchscreen from another provider.

Blackberry's business model was based on giving carriers a product that could be used on their networks. Its leaders persisted in their belief that the mobile offering had to be tailored to the carrier networks, which is why Blackberry co-chairman and co-CEO Mike Lazaridis were convinced all the offerings on the iPhone made it unworkable: the networks would never be big enough. What happened is that the success of the iPhone made the carriers expand their networks!

Blackberry also persisted in leaving small screens and keyboards on their phones. Only when Blackberry's carrier, Verizon, insisted that Blackberry develop touchscreen technology did the Canadian mobile giant try to modernize its phones. However, in part due to an overly aggressive deadline set by Verizon, the Blackberry touch-screen technology was clunky and bug-ridden. Once the undisputed smartphone champion, Blackberry would become completely irrelevant in the mobile phone market.

THE GREATEST CHALLENGE

Although wildly diverse, every story in this chapter has the same, single lesson:

Know when to stop.

Know when to stop

... fighting the war.

... climbing a mountain that you'll never survive.

… calling a prospect to point that he no longer wants to work with you.

… manufacturing your beloved legacy product that is fast becoming obsolete.

The words are simple, but as the stories in this chapter illustrate, stopping can indeed be, as Rockwell notes for leadership, the greatest challenge.

Especially for those who have the persistence required to succeed. After all, many people succeed because when others stop, they don't. Which is why resisting the dark side of persistence is so difficult. It sounds like a mixed message: persistence is knowing that you can't succeed if you stop.

But sometimes you have to stop.

FROM DARKNESS TO LIGHT: THE STORY OF SANGE SHERPA

Most of the stories in this chapter illustrate the dark side of persistence, when persistence becomes obsession or obstinacy, often leading to unfortunate, if not tragic, consequences. The story of my dear friend Sange Sherpa and his first client is another story about foolish obstinacy (on the part of the client), but it becomes a story of amazing persistence and the refusal to give up in the face of obstacles that few people have endured.

When I met Sange Sherpa, he was a 19-year-old Nepal native who had dreamed his whole of life of being a guide on Mt. Everest. Despite his young age, Sange was the main provider for his five siblings—his mother died tragically when Sange was 14, and his father had little interest in providing what was needed for his children to survive.

Like others who are raised in abject poverty, with little to no educational opportunity, and bearing the weight of providing for a fractured family, Sange knew that to rise above his circumstances he would have to excel in the one particular skill that he learned: high mountain climbing. He recognized intuitively as a young boy that the way to pull himself and his siblings out of his village's poverty was staring him in the face every day, and it was 29,000 feet high.

In the spring of 2017, I organized a group to travel to Mt. Everest base camp, trekking through the Khumbu Valley in the Sagamartha National Park, Nepal. Ours was a group of 19 assembled friends and family. My climbing partner, Tom, and I were intent on summiting Mt. Everest; a few in the group would join us on an acclimatization climb to the summit of Lobuche; the rest were trekking to base camp.

I first met Sange as we departed from Lukla for Phakding on the first leg of the trek to base camp. It's about a 40-mile trek from the village of Lukla to base camp, completed over seven days. Sange was there every step of the way: helping people in the group in any way he could, such as taking backpacks off the shoulders of slower trekkers. Every time our group would stop and rest, Sange would be there pouring tea, telling us to drink and hydrate, repeatedly saying that it would help avoid altitude sickness. Always polite and encouraging as we continued on the dusty trail into thinner air, he never seemed to rest and was constantly checking on our condition.

I was really struck by what a respectful, surprisingly strong, great teenager he was.

Over the course of many days, our group climbed higher and higher, passing through incredible mountain passes and staying each night in a new village in one of the local teahouses. This trek can be a grind at times: each day climbing higher, with altitude pressing the lungs and mind; an unfamiliar diet combined with loss of appetite; sleep sometimes impossible to find; and less than sanitary bathroom facilities. It wears everyone down both physically and mentally, but each morning Sange was there with a ready smile and a cup of tea. Group attitude is sometimes determined by the smallest things, and Sange's unfailingly pleasant outlook kept our group amazingly positive.

After finally arriving at Everest base camp, in various stages of health, Tom and I said an emotional goodbye to our friends and family who helicoptered from base camp back to Kathmandu, and thus our expedition truly began.

For any expedition, there's an acclimatization period required to prepare the body for surviving at extreme altitudes. And as part of this acclimatization, we climbed up a 20,000-foot peak called Lobuche that lays shadow to its namesake village. Lobuche is a perfect peak for training and acclimatization. It offers the most spectacular views of Mt. Everest. It also provides a varied terrain of rock, ice, glaciers, rope travel, and crevasses—perfect for preparing us to climb Everest. At times, we were wading through thigh-deep snow, post-holing as our legs sunk deep into powder. A rock scramble section led to the glacier that ultimately delivered us to the summit ridge. Having successfully climbed multiple peaks all over the world and knowing the value of a good guide, it was encouraging to have Sange as our lead guide for Lobuche, who, although young, led us successfully to the summit and back down to base camp. At that point, Sange's duties with us were finished. I said my heartfelt goodbye as we'd spent the better part of two weeks together bonding only as you can when working together as a team in extreme environments.

Sange now shifted his attention to Mt. Everest, where he was going to be a rescue guide at the highest camp on the mountain—Camp 4 at 26,000 feet. If anybody needed assistance, he would be there to come to their rescue. His plan was to be a rescue guide this year and hopefully next year get an opportunity to guide a climber on his/her summit attempt.

Even though Sange and I were on the same mountain, our paths diverged. My unsuccessful expedition, which I described in the Introduction, continued. All the while, Sange's journey was running parallel to mine. On May 17, 2017, I was at Camp 2, hoping against hope to make another attempt. I petitioned to Tom, Larry, and Brandon to make another attempt with me, but they were too exhausted and headed back down to base camp. I was praying that the weather would clear enough for another summit attempt.

It was very disheartening to continuously hear the poor weather reports, and to have been so close to the summit yet knowing that I may have to abandon. I remember sitting alone in the dining tent at Camp 2 when I heard someone walk in behind me. I didn't have the desire to turn around to see who came in, so I sat there, looking away, when suddenly I heard a familiar voice say: "David dai!" (*Dai* is a term of respect used with someone who is familiar to you.) I turned around to see Sange's beaming smile, and he excitedly told me that he had a client for the summit—a Pakistani doctor. It was so refreshing to see a familiar face and also to see someone so excited about getting his chance to be a guide to the summit of Everest. Having a summit on your resume gives Sherpas credibility and job security for years to come. It's also a high-status mark in their community.

What I didn't find out until later was that two other guides and a guide company had turned down this Pakistani climber, a retired 60-year-old army Colonel. With media running across Pakistan tracking his progress as a minor celebrity, much was on the line for his personal success and his countrymen. These guides and the guide company had determined that he was completely unfit—that he was just too slow, too inexperienced, and shouldn't be high on the mountain.

Meanwhile, waiting at Camp 2, I still held out hope that I would be able to have a summit window. Unfortunately, on the morning of May 19th, Lhakpa Gelu Sherpa delivered the final blow over the radio and informed me the weather would be the same for several days. With no desire to reach the same spot at the South Summit only to be turned away again, I abandoned my climb and descended the mountain, heading home.

I just arrived back home with the fog of the devastating expedition still clouding my mind when I got a text message from my friend, Doug Madsen, who had climbed Lobuche with us. The message said, "If you ever wondered if you should have turned back or if you have any doubt of listening to your guides, have you heard what happened to Sange?" My heart sank as any news about Sherpas on Everest is rarely ever good news.

The day that I turned back—when my base camp manager said the weather was uncertain and I decided not to take a chance on uncertain weather—was the day that Sange and the Pakistani doctor attempted the summit. It was also the day that four climbers would lose their lives on Everest.

Due to the Pakistani doctor's extremely slow pace, Sange made the decision to start out around 5 p.m. from Camp 4, a full four hours before the time regular guiding companies start with their clients. They advanced very slowly. The Pakistani doctor himself was moving extremely slowly, and he had Sange carrying more oxygen than he should have been because their team had not stashed oxygen up high, which is a requirement for well-organized expeditions.

After climbing for nine hours, Sange realized that they had no chance of making the summit with time to safely descend, and told his client that they needed to turn back; at the pace they were going, he explained to the Pakistani doctor, they were going to run out of oxygen.

He refused to listen and demanded they continue with the climb. An hour later, Sange again said they "must" turn back, and again, he refused, telling Sange, "I've come too far, I've paid too much royalty, I'm going to keep going."

Faced with an impossible decision, Sange had a choice to make. A choice no 19-year-old should have to make alone, while cold, exhausted, and on the world's highest mountain. He could turn back and leave his client on the mountain—an action that would have been justifiable because the Pakistani doctor was refusing to listen and to take the guidance of a more experienced mountaineer whom he willingly engaged to lead him on his climb. But Sange knew that if he left him alone, the colonel would certainly die, and he thought to himself, "My life is no more important than his."

So, against his better judgment, he stayed with the Pakistani doctor, who continued his excruciatingly slow climb toward the summit. They eventually reached the "Balcony," a flat portion about 1,700 feet from the summit (the same place where Shriya Shah had died in the story that opened this chapter). There, Sange switched out his client's oxygen tank, but not his own, opting to hold it in reserve for the climb down.

Meanwhile, the already deteriorating weather took a turn for the worse. The strong wind quickly became a gale force, slowing down the already slow doctor even more, and causing the already frigid temperatures to plummet. As the two men started the final 1,500 feet climb to the summit, through the infamous Death Zone, their oxygen masks were freezing, their goggles were frosted over, and the temperature only continued to sink. The Death Zone has earned its name. No person can survive in the exposure of the Death Zone for more than 48 hours. Over 300 people have died on Mt. Everest, and many of them remain in the Death Zone, since it is dangerous to try to bring down the bodies; you unfortunately get used to walking by corpses as you head to the summit—and hope that you will never be one of those corpses, partially entombed in the snow year after year.

THE DARK SIDE OF PERSISTENCE

Sange and the Pakistani doctor (who was still moving at death march pace and refusing to retreat) finally made it through the Hillary Step and reached the summit at 3:30 p.m., completely exhausted from the climbing, the cold, and the altitude. A summit photo was taken— Sange said later he was not sure the photo would be good because he was already starting to feel dizzy and his vision was getting blurry—and then they retreated from the summit. Less than 300 feet into the descent, the Pakistani doctor sat down and didn't respond to Sange's demands. Sange also decided to sit down and immediately slipped into unconsciousness. They both lay there, inert at the South Summit, as the sun began to set. A long silent night passed for both men as any remaining life began to drain from their bodies. Around 4:00 a.m. the next morning, the next day's climbers attempting the summit began to pass the unmoving climbers. It was assumed by all that they were dead.

HOW OUR BODIES FIGHT HYPOTHERMIA

Before we continue with Sange's story, you need to know a little about one of the fiercest enemies of the mountaineer: hypothermia.

There is no greater example of a body automatically fighting for survival then the example of hypothermia. Hypothermia is the term for a dangerous drop in body temperature. The normal body temperature is 98.6 degrees Fahrenheit. That's the temperature for all the component parts of our body to operate: for our blood to circulate, our lungs to breathe, our heart to pump, and our brain to think, remember, and transform decisions to act (to walk, for example) into physical actions (moving our legs). All of this massive amount of activity, mostly ignored and yet vital for life, will start to wind down if our body temperature starts to drop...

But our bodies will not give up. They will fight. If the temperature drops below 89° F, your body no longer has the energy to pump blood, so it makes a decision: it will pump blood to vital organs only, and the far reaches of the body—our hands, our feet—will have to do without. It implements this decision through a process called vasoconstriction, which refers to the narrowing of our veins and arteries, which limits blood flow. The body also raises the hairs on our skin, trying to create an insulating "fur" for us—erect hair will trap more warm air against the skin. In truth, it's not very effective, but worth a shot.

If our body temperature drops down to 87° F, we start to shiver. This is not the little shivering that we might feel on a cold night. This shiver is more like convulsions, caused by the body very quickly contracting and expanding our muscles to create warmth. When I was climbing in Russia and didn't take the time to put on a down coat or consume warm liquids, my body dipped below 87° F, and the uncontrolled convulsions began—convulsions that didn't stop until I put on my down parka and drank some hot tea and my body warmed enough to stop them.

Eventually, the muscles needed for these warming actions—the shivering and the vasoconstriction that diverts all the blood to our vital organs—become exhausted and fail. The result: blood floods back to our arms, hands, and feet, abandoning the vital organs including our brain. Our brain starts to lose its ability to function properly. Confusion, hallucinations, deafness—these are all signs that the cold has reached the brain. And when we start to feel warm as a result of the blood rushing to our extremities, our brain cannot logically process this sudden warming correctly. And so, in this deep confusion, our addled brains tell us to undress, despite the fact that the cold is destroying us on the inside—a phenomenon known as *paradoxical undressing*.

As our body temperature slides further down to 85° F, there is no more energy left, and our body falls into a coma, and we begin to die. The heart stops. The brain dies. Ironically, because of the frigid temperatures, the dying occurs slowly—so slowly that sometimes freezing bodies on the brink of death can be rescued.

HEROES

As Sange lay in the snow, completely inert, climbers walked past what they considered was another climber who would never make it off the mountain. Sange was not dead, however. He was even partially conscious and could hear the climbers' crampons as they were walking nearby. But he could not move and he could not cry out. So, he just laid there and, in his own words, describes what he heard and felt:

There were many climbers going to the summit. I was feeling very hungry and thirsty, my water bottle was frozen, and no matter how hard I tried, I was not able to move my hands and body at all; there was no sense in both my hands. Soon I realized my hands were completely frostbitten, I was very hopeless and tired that I could have easily closed my eyes and become a permanent member of the mountain. It would have been very peaceful rather than suffering. I was waiting for death when I could feel my body cold as ice; breathing and heartbeat were very slow. The climbers going to the summit didn't even approach me as I was like a dead body. I was unable to move and speak properly. At this point, I needed help. And I gave it to God. I surrendered. I kept praying to God and at that moment, I witnessed a miracle. God himself came to help me in a form of friends Ang Tsering Lama and his other Sherpa friends from Sherpa Khangri Outdoor. Luckily, they recognized me. At first they thought I was dead.

Ang Tsering Lama and his Sherpa crew are, in my view, true heroes. As soon as Ang Tsering realized Sange was alive, he sprang into action. Ang was guiding his own crew, with his own clients who went up the mountain ahead; he decided to forego his own summit bid to save these two individuals.

He and the other Sherpas he recruited immediately put their oxygen on the two climbers. Sange was unresponsive but alive. They tied him to a makeshift litter, tied the litter to a rope, and then, foot-by-foot, they excruciatingly lowered him to Camp 4, a truly exhausting and wildly dangerous process which became the highest rescue in Everest history. Once he arrived at Camp 4, a doctor from Wyoming treated him as best she could. He was then lowered to Camp 3. The Pakistani doctor could no longer continue, so in an effort to evacuate and save his life, the brave helicopter pilot performed a 'long line' cable rescue. Since the helicopter couldn't land, they lowered a cable to hook into the harness of the Pakistani doctor to secure him, flying him down the Western CWM, past the Khumbu Icefall and down to basecamp where they could safely move him into the helicopter to transport him to Kathmandu. Meanwhile, Sange was now able to move, albeit slowly, into Camp 2, where a helicopter was able to land and transfer him to Kathmandu.

It is a miracle, as Sange says, that the two did not die on the mountain. If Ang did not check on the men instead of assuming that they were dead, and then attempt something that had never been attempted—a rescue within a few hundred feet of the summit— the Pakistani doctor's insistence on continuing the climb in spite of the warnings of Sange would have cost both men their lives.

Instead, his obstinacy cost them their fingers—and more damage was done to Sange's hands than the Pakistani doctor's. At some point from when Sange collapsed at the South Summit to his rescue, his gloves were lost completely, exposing his hands to the harsh elements. As a result, all of Sange's fingers were frozen solid.

The next phase of the Sange's journey began with his arrival at the hospital in Kathmandu, a phase in which Sange's amazing persistence not just to recover, but also to recover without ever losing his optimism and his good nature, is nothing short of astounding.

Meanwhile, the Pakistani doctor continues to demonstrate disheartening selfishness and seems to be completely oblivious to the fact that his foolishness, his obstinate persistence, is the reason that the two lost their hands and could have easily lost their lives. In Pakistan, he is treated as a hero and was awarded the President's Medal for Pride of Performance, all without ever thanking those who saved his life. He is almost flippant when talking about what he put himself and Sange through by refusing to listen to those who knew better. In one article, he is quoted as saying, "By just sacrificing our fingers, we've become celebrities."

"Just sacrificing our fingers." What an ignorant statement. By nearly sacrificing the life of an innocent young man who decidedly put his life on the line for yours, by making the insensible, selfish decision to continue when experienced voices were saying otherwise, by attempting a climb without making the effort to get into the required condition or gain the necessary experience, you get your articles in the Pakistani papers—and this makes you proud?

The Pakistani doctor is the epitome of the dark side of persistence: the foolish, obsessive, or tragic side of not knowing when to turn back or when to stop, not knowing when to listen to the reasonable warnings of others rather than persisting in your own inexperience.

BACK TO THE LIGHT: SANGE IN COLORADO

The story of Sange Sherpa does not end at the hospital in Kathmandu. In fact, it is only the beginning of a journey that exemplifies the best of persistence of the human spirit.

Sange messaged me from Kathmandu, fearing that the surgeons in Nepal would remove his hands. I told Sange I didn't know how to comment on their recommendation, but I did know we needed to get him to the U.S. for the best possible solution.

I started a GoFundMe campaign to help defray the enormous costs of treating Sange in the U.S., raising tens of thousands of dollars in support.

On learning of the extensive damage to Sange's hands, word spread, and help from the best orthopedic surgeons in the world arrived. And one of the best surgeons for the repair of hands is Dr. Randall Viola, at the Steadman Clinic in Vail, Colorado. Viola is the head physician of the U.S. Alpine Ski Team.

But this is, of course, only a beginning; Sange's tragic yet inspiring story caught the attention of others, and the largest part of his treatment was covered by the Kees Brenninkmeyer Foundation, which offers amazing support to alpine guides, patrollers, or instructors who are injured and need surgery to continue their careers. The foundation became involved through an individual who has been one of the key figures in Sange's recovery, a Sherpa who was born in Nepal and now lives in Colorado. He had connections to the foundation and was able to get them on board immediately.

That was the first step. It was only after we had secured the foundation's support for Sange's surgeries could we think about bringing him over. Without the financial commitment of the foundation, there would have been no reason for him to come to the U.S.

Unfortunately, we then ran into a series of bureaucratic problems, as the U.S. consulate refused to issue him a visa. We had congressmen, other officials, everyone we could think of trying to convince the consulate to let him come, without success, all the while concerned that infection would be setting into Sange's hands.

At some point, the doctor from Wyoming reached out, and asked how she could help. At the same time, we got a message from the embassy that they are willing to give Sange a visa if someone was willing to come to Kathmandu and accompany him back. The doctor from Wyoming immediately flew to Kathmandu and took care of him as they flew to Denver, where the local Sherpa picked him up and took him to Vail; three days later, Sange had his first surgery.

Over the course of more than a dozen surgeries, Dr. Viola removed on Sange's right hand the index and pinky fingers down to the center of the hand, the two middle fingers down to the top of the hand, and the thumb past the first knuckle. On Sange's left hand, the index finger was removed down near the wrist with the fingers removed to the base and the thumb below the knuckle. After each finger amputation, there was a process of sewing his hand into his abdomen to help in the healing process. Once the right hand was healed, into the abdomen went the left hand.

As if losing all of his fingers was not enough, all of these surgeries required skin to be transplanted from his abdomen, skin that is used to fold over his open wounds. So Sange's whole abdomen is grafted and spliced. Dr. Viola and staff continued to work their talents with the best procedures by grafting and constructing Sange's hip bone and screwing this bone to the two middle "fingers" on each hand, which has now provided Sange with dexterity and the ability to grab that would have never been possible through surgeries in Nepal.

As I write this, Sange continues to be an incredible inspiration. When I traveled to visit him in the hospital in Vail after his first surgery, he had a continuous smile on his face. Today, in every visit out to our home and every video conversation, he continues to be upbeat, he continues to smile, he continues to be totally humble. He doesn't view life in tragedy, but continues to view life with triumph.

And he continues to plan for the future. This tragedy is not going to stop him. One reason is that incredibly, he doesn't have any regrets. When they first took him off the mountain, Sange said he wouldn't change a thing—that he would stay with the Pakistani doctor again, because he would never let another person die.

Sange is not saddled with regret, blame, or anger, and that is one of the most important characteristics of those who persist. They don't get blown back by the past, they lean in to the future. I think of Sange's words when he talks about lying immobile on the mountain: *I could have easily closed my eyes and become a permanent member of the mountain. It would have been very peaceful rather than suffering.* But Sange had the will to survive, and he will have to thrive despite the hurdles he will continue to face.

There are a lot of people who have been involved in Sange's story: the heroic Ang Tsering Lama and his team, who saved Sange's life; the physician who treated him at Camp 4 and who accompanied him from Kathmandu to the U.S.; the local Sherpa who has made the connections and set up the network for the surgeries and looks out for his interests; the brilliant Dr. Viola, who is giving Sange every opportunity to recover as much function as he can; and the wonderful foundation offering vital financial support, making all of this possible.

And someone I haven't mentioned yet, a kind and generous widow in Colorado who has donated her time, funds, home, and network of support contacts for Sange. She was continuously involved in the care of Sange, driving him to his appointments, working with him on his English, and enrolling him in local running and biking clubs. She made it possible for Sange to travel back after his visa expired and to return to the U.S. under a multi-year extension.

While there are many heroes involved with this story, without doubt, the greatest hero is Sange himself. He is the epitome of persistence, and the proof is not only what he has accomplished, and what he will accomplish—the proof is also in all of the people that I just mentioned who are humble and grateful to be able to help this young man. Because one of the signs of the truly persistent is their inspiration to others.

And I've never known anyone more inspirational than Sange Sherpa.

CHAPTER SEVEN

DON'T ALMOST

Regret is such a short word…and yet is stretches on forever.
— Ranata Suzuki

In early summer of 2017, with the heavy weight of coming up short on Everest a few months earlier still pressing on my mind, I traveled to Mammoth Lakes, California for my wife's family reunion. We rented paddleboards from the lake shop for the day and voyaged to the far side of the lake where we had set up camp. Time approached to return the boards for the 4:00 p.m. cutoff just as a strong headwind picked up, which meant that paddling the board would take longer than I anticipated. We had the option of throwing the boards in our pickup truck, which was staged nearby, and driving them around the lake, an option that would certainly get the paddleboards back in time. However, I was determined to paddle into the wind and across the lake. When I stated my intent to paddle, my concerned daughter said, "Dad, are you sure you can make it in time?" Responding to her question, my well-meaning uncle in-law said, "Of course he can, he *almost* climbed Mt. Everest."

In his compliment of my ability to make it across the lake, the word *almost* sharply stung. I was the *almost* guy. Almost reached the rooftop of the world. Almost completed the Seven Summits ... *Almost*. The support from friends and family comforting me by saying that I "basically" reached the top and "it's really the same as summiting, you had 99 percent of the total experience," was offered in sincerity, but fell flat. I couldn't sweep the failure to reach the top from my soul. I knew *almost* would haunt me forever. Would *almost* be my mountaineering legacy, my final chapter? Could I accept that?

Rationalization is the enemy of persistence. Rationalization is convincing yourself that you are okay with failure, you are okay with giving up. It means that you tell yourself that you'll be "fine" abandoning your climb, your goals, your dreams. "I can't finish my degree, I have two kids now," you tell yourself. "Losing those final 15 pounds will be impossible, I'm just big boned." Or we fixate on who we've always been: "That's just who I am. I can't change it."

Almost rarely brings fulfillment. In fact, *almost* can be, in many instances, worse than outright failure. Just ask silver medalists in the Olympic Games. Being selected to represent your country is a dream for any athlete. Most runners, swimmers, biathletes, gymnasts, and athletes in scores of other sports dream of making it to the Olympic games. Only a few superior athletes are ever selected to their national Olympic teams, and of those, only a small fraction actually contends for medals. By that reasoning, silver medalists are among the absolute elite in their respective sports.

Surprisingly, different studies comparing the emotions of silver medalists to bronze medalists show that, in fact, winning the silver (*almost* reaching gold) often leaves the silver medalists feeling worse than those who won the bronze medal.

In one study, the researchers asked a group of undergraduate students to watch videos from the 1992 Summer Olympics and rate on a scale of 1 ("agony") to 10 ("ecstasy") the emotional reactions of the athletes when the medal results were announced. The results: Those who won a silver medal were shown to be much less happy (earning an average score of 4.8) than those who learned that they had just won a bronze medal (they earned an average score of 7.1 on the happiness scale!). A later study of 2006 Olympic judo wrestlers showed a similar same set of reactions at the end of their matches: gold medalists were exultant, most of the bronze medalists were smiling, while the reactions of silver medalists ranged from showing no emotion to scowling in disgust.

Why should silver medalists be so unsatisfied? The reason is that they *almost* reached gold. Many bronze medalists, on the other hand, are delighted because they were likely never contenders for a gold medal, or were in fear that they wouldn't medal at all. Thus, being selected to represent their countries and then bringing home a medal sends them over the moon. So, you have the ironic situation of third-place finishers being very happy and second-place finishers being unhappy ... all because of the affliction of *almost*.

This is the curse that will follow you through life if you give up when you are close to success, if you give up just out of fatigue or frustration, even though the goal and gold may be near. If you concede and stop taking that next step.

Don't give up. Your brain may try to rationalize your defeat, but your heart will never accept it.

HE COULD HAVE BEEN A LEGEND

Edmund Hillary and Sherpa Tensing Norgay are, of course, the first climbers to reach the summit of Mt. Everest. That spectacular feat earned Hillary and Norgay worldwide fame that continues to this day. They are without doubt the most well-known mountain climbers in history and an inspiration to many—examples of determination and courage to anyone struggling to achieve their quest.

And yet, only three days before Hillary and Norgay stepped on that peak, two other climbers, named Tom Bourdillon and Charles Evans, came within 300 feet of being the first men to reach the summit of Everest. For those two climbers, those 300 feet of icy, rocky ridge that they were unable to breach meant the difference between achieving immortality as great mountain climbers and being obscure footnotes in mountain climbing history.

Only 300 feet. So close.

For the rest of their lives, Bourdillon and Evans would regret their failure to finish that climb on that afternoon of May 26, 1953.

Bourdillon and Evans blamed their equipment, exhaustion, and the 40-foot rock formation separating them from the summit and which they argued was impossible to climb. We all carry around what I call our blamethrower, and it's fueled by our excuses: "My territory just doesn't have the right leads," "I don't have time to exercise" "If my dad only hugged me more as a child." We torch anything in our path with our blamethrower in hopes it will justify our current excuse. And the funny thing is, the excuses and blame are usually correct, but they're totally irrelevant because excuses will never eliminate that 40-foot rock formation standing between us and our summit.

Bourdillon and Evans were part of a six-man British expedition team led by James Hunt, and including Hillary and Tenzing. Hunt had decided that Bourdillon and Evans would be the first two-man team from the expedition to make the first final ascent to the peak of Everest. As author Mick Conefrey explains in his book, *Everest 1953: The Epic Story of the First Ascent*, Hunt has chosen his teams carefully. Bourdillon was a brilliant climber, known for taking the most difficult routes in the Alps. He was a conqueror of peaks. Evans was a different kind of climber. He enjoyed discovering uncharted territories more than "bagging" peaks. He was committed to the expedition's success but not at any risk. Hunt believed, Conefrey writes, that Evans would temper Bourdillon's determination.

Hunt was right. With their oxygen running low due to problems with their masks, Conefrey described how Evans argued that they needed to turn back. It's possible that had they continued, they would have died, so the decision to turn back was likely a wise one. Still, the decision was a bitter disappointment for Bourdillon. "We should have gone on, we should have gone on," he kept repeating when they returned to the South Col. As Conefrey writes, "Charles was relieved to have made it back alive and cheered by the warm welcome of the others, but Tom spent the night churning over the events of the day. If only he had prepared the oxygen sets better; if only he had ignored Charles's suggestion to change cylinders; if only he'd gone on alone."

Tom Bourdillon knew that he missed out on the chance of entering mountain climbing immortality. Tragically, Bourdillon's regret was short-lived as he died in a mountain-climbing accident only a few years later.

CRUTCH OR MOTIVATION? THE POWER OF COUNTERFACTUALS

Counterfactual thinking is thinking of an alternative fact that's related to a fact. I know that's a mouthful, but we do it all the time! For example, on one trip up the Khumbu Icefall, an avalanche broke near us. I could have said to myself, "I almost was caught in that avalanche." The bare fact—the actual event that happened—is that the avalanche missed me. With counterfactual thinking, you created another interpretation of the event: I *almost* was swept away in the slide. And that's just one possible interpretation. Here are other examples of counterfactual thinking that could relate to the avalanche in the Khumbu Icefall:

If I had been going faster, I would have been caught in the avalanche.

I was lucky to miss the avalanche. It's only because of our slow methodical pace that we missed it.

We almost paid with our lives! If the Icefall Doctors would have laid a better route, we would have been removed from that avalanche path.

These are just a few examples taken from the one incident. You can see how you come up with counterfactuals in everyday scenarios. Psychologists have names for the different categories of counterfactuals (upward evaluation counterfactuals, additive counterfactuals, and so on), but the terminology is beyond the discussion of this book.

The main point is that the counterfactuals you choose to create related to what's happening can have a significant impact on your persistence because they change your mindset. Why are the Olympic silver medalists unhappy and the bronze medalists delighted? Because of their counterfactuals! What are the silver medalists thinking?

"I failed to get a gold medal."

In contrast, what are the bronze medalists thinking?

"I'm not going home empty-handed. I got a medal!"

Objectively, the silver medalists are more successful than the bronze medalists. None of the athletes would argue with that *fact*. But because of their *counterfactual* thinking, the silver medalists in the study consider themselves failures and the bronze medalists consider themselves wildly successful!

This power of counterfactuals on your feelings or mindset is why counterfactuals can decide whether you persist or give up.

Imagine that several candidates are vying for a promotion. Eventually, the choice is whittled down to two candidates. When the announcements are made, the CEO informs the candidates that the choice was very close.

The *losing* candidate could think the following:

"I failed to get that promotion."

"I did my best and almost got the promotion, so I'm still proud of myself."

"I didn't get the promotion, but at least I am fortunate not to get fired like Ryan." (Ryan is a friend of the candidate who got fired from another firm after 20 years.)

Which of these three counterfactual options is going to make the candidate work even harder to get the next promotion and get closer to his goal of reaching the C-suite?

Let's say we have a losing candidate named Becky, who thinks, "I almost got that promotion, so I'm still proud of myself" or "I didn't get the promotion, but at least I am fortunate not to get fired like Ryan." She's disappointed but not devastated. She did her best, and things could be worse. The next time there's a promotion open, she'll try her best and see what happens. But if she doesn't get it, well, things could be worse.

On the other hand, a losing candidate named Jeff thinks, "I failed to get that promotion." Jeff is deeply unhappy. He's a failure. And by so little. The next time a promotion comes, this candidate is going to launch himself into the effort: he's not going to let another opportunity slip away. This candidate has the mountain mindset.

Let's put this psychology in mountaineering terms. On my very first mountaineering peak, there are many times I wanted to turn back on Mt. Rainier. There are many times when "reality" was not cooperating. But if I didn't make the summit, I was defeated. I wouldn't think to myself, "I almost made the summit, that's pretty good." I would think to myself, "I failed to make the summit." The research shows—in psychological terminology— that thinking the second way is why I was able to climb the Seven Summits.

The bottom line: reality is not objective but subjective. Depending on how you approach the "fact," you will be either really motivated to persist and succeed, or generally satisfied with the way things are and not feel any urgency in changing the status quo. If that's the way you feel, you are not going to be able to overcome the barriers that bar your way to success.

DON'T ASSUME YOU'LL BE BACK

When our team turned back 300 feet from the summit of Everest in 2017, it was an absolute disappointment. Even then, as I was taking my final steps off the mountain and out of Everest base camp for good, I knew I couldn't let it end this way. Would my Seven Summits legacy be cut short by 300 feet? After our family reunion, where my uncle in-law said I *almost* climbed Everest, that word continued to plague my thoughts. Mere weeks after leaving the mountain, the arduous climb still fresh in my mind and my body still recovering, I decided to open a conversation with my friend Tom about going back. The mental and physical toll of over a month spent in Nepal weren't easy to dismiss, and the strength it would take to start again on the path of mental and physical preparation and what would lie ahead was unnerving. Tom, being the climber he is, soon warmed to the idea.

After putting the word out, Larry couldn't climb again as he'd miss his daughter's 16th birthday, and Brandon was going through his divorce. We ended up with two other climbing friends, Fabian and Dan, joining us for our 2018 Everest expedition. Planning and training began again in earnest. With a competent and confident climbing team, I did what I usually do: get everything in place for a successful expedition attempt and then ask for the wife pass. Having the conversation to ask my wife to jeopardize everything and allow me to head to Everest the first time was daunting. But to ask again!?! My wife understood the depression that had been self-imposed by not reaching the top. She recognized that I had been a different person during that summer. A different person until we decided we were going to take another shot at the top the following year. Could I have lived with not summiting Everest? Sure. We gave it everything, and the weather turned us back. But I couldn't live with the dull ache of almost. If I was afforded another chance, I was going to take it.

With her blessing, we made preparations for our climb. Eventually, we were geared up and ready to go. We were going to get another chance to reach the top of the world. Not everybody gets a second chance at their summit, and that's another important reason not to "almost:" You may not know it, but that may be your only shot.

When he was just 23 years old, future pro football Hall of Famer Dan Marino led his team, the Miami Dolphins, to the 1985 Super Bowl. It was just his second year in the league. In that year, he threw 48 touchdown passes, leading the Dolphins to a 14-2 regular season record and earning him the Most Valuable Player award. After dismantling the Seattle Seahawks and the Pittsburgh Steelers (which had been his hometown team), the Dolphins faced the San Francisco 49ers in the Super Bowl. And lost.

Marino was disappointed, but he also knew that he had many years of football ahead of him and that he would be back to play for the championship again. As he told the *Miami Herald* in 2015, he was positive he was going to be back in the Super Bowl, probably more than once, and would no doubt win at least once.

Marino was wrong. In his 17 seasons with the Dolphins, he made the playoffs 10 times. But he never returned to the Super Bowl.

As the famous line in the play *Hamilton* says, "I'm not throwing away my shot." Treat every summit attempt like it's your only one. Never assume that you'll have another chance to reach your dream. Never assume that there will be a "better time" to take the risk. Dan Marino is one of the greatest quarterbacks in NFL history. But he never got a second chance to win a Super Bowl, and it's the one regret of his career.

WHY YOU'LL REGRET *NOT* DOING SOMETHING

There is no doubt my life would have turned out very differently had I never taken that first step up Mt. Rainier, accepting that challenge of my coworker. There would be no Kilimanjaro trekking and safari company, no lifelong friendships with Brandon, Larry, Dan, Fabian, Lhakpa, Sange, Gyaljen, and countless others. No touching the highest mountains on every continent, no derived benefits from constantly challenging myself in the most extreme environments, perhaps not the same financial freedom and living life on my terms. The list could go on and on.

Psychologists say that there are two types of regret: regret over things you did, and regrets over things you did not do. Psychological studies show that there's a big difference between how we react to these two types of regrets. When you regret something that you did, there is an immediate or near-immediate big reaction—you're angry at yourself or disgusted or distressed. However, the regret dissipates relatively quickly. The regret you really hang on to is regretting something you have *not* done. That's the kind of regret that can last years, even a lifetime.

The reason that regrets over what you didn't do will haunt you for a long time is that there is usually or often something you can do about the action you regret, but there is nothing you can about the non-action you regret. In a study about regret conducted by Allianz, the life insurance company, nearly one-third of the adults surveyed regretted some of the major decisions they made in life, including their professions and where they worked. Not having traveled more and not having been "more adventurous" was one of the top regrets cited in the survey. The study, called "The Gift of Time," then asked the respondents what they would do if they had 30 more years to live. Most would say they would travel or live somewhere else, or just plain "take more risks."

But there may be something you can do even for the regrets of action not taken. Psychologists Shai Davidai and Tom Gilovich use self-discrepancy theory to offer a way out of regrets. According to self-discrepancy theory, developed by psychologist Tory

Higgins, most of us have an *ideal* self—who and what we'd really like to be—and an *ought* self—what we feel we should be. And then, of course, there's the *actual* self. Personality tests fail when someone answers them as their ideal self rather than their actual self. Higgins's theory talks about the psychological problems that result when there's a discrepancy between the actual self and either the ought or the ideal selves. For Davidai and Gilovich, when you regret an action taken, you're focusing on a gap between actual self and ought self: what you actually did and what you should have done. Actual vs. ought tension is going to lead to the *hot* emotions: being angry, disgusted, or distressed.

When you regret not taking an action, the tension is between your actual self and your ideal self: what you could have done and what you actually did. Actual vs. ideal tension doesn't lead to the same hot emotions as actual vs. ought. Instead of being angry or distressed, you are going to be sad or disappointed—what psychologists call cool emotions.

Why does hot vs. cool emotions make a difference? Because you don't deal with cool emotions. You don't react to them. You repress them, you live with them, and that's why your regrets over something you never did stick around. You have filed those regrets deep inside you.

In other words, when you are dealing with a gap between your actual and your *ought* self, you're motivated to take action and fix this gap. But when you're dealing with a gap between your actual self and your ideal self, you're more likely to say, "Well, that's the ideal, but that's not reality, what can I do?"

But that's Davidai and Gilovich's point: Don't give up on your ideal self. First of all, because that longing for the ideal self is not going to go away, even if you think it will. And second, because there's no reason that only the ought self gaps are fixable. You can't go back in time, but you can bring out that ideal self that you've stashed away and decide: how can I get as close to this ideal self as possible?

In short, persist in achieving the ideal self. Psychologists have explained why we don't persist in trying to achieve this goal. Now that you know that psychologically we are not motivated to achieve the ideal self in the same way that we're motivated to achieve the ought self, you have to push yourself even more to persist in achieving the ideal self.

This is the whole lesson of the Gift of Life study. Given 30 more years to live, people are going to forget about the ought self and focus on the ideal self.

So, bottom line, don't accept having done what you ought to have done. Don't stop until you've reached your ideal self, because if you do stop and if you do give up, you will be stuffing all those regrets into the attic of your consciousness, and they will continue to echo.

BATTLE FOR GRADUATE SCHOOL: THE DEAN GIVES IN ... AFTER ELEVEN MONTHS!

I could have fallen into an 'ought to' when I got the unexpected chance to pursue a graduate degree. With a wife, daughters, and career, there's never a convenient time to pursue a graduate degree. I didn't finish my undergraduate degree until I was 26, so the idea that I ought to go back to school was not an exciting proposition. But with a job that was willing to provide tuition reimbursement, it would have been wasted money and a wasted opportunity if I didn't at least try to get a higher degree.

My work reimbursement also covered a GMAT study course for the required entrance exam for any Masters of Business Administration. I studied, took the test, and received an average score. I paid (through company reimbursement) a private tutor meeting for four hours a week for four weeks to increase my GMAT score only to take it again receiving a lower score!

Knowing I needed to attend a different school from my undergrad at University of Utah, I submitted applications to the only two schools that made sense for me to attend—Westminster College in Salt Lake City or Utah State University—and was quickly rejected by both.

The rejection letters, which are still filed next to me at my desk to this day, said, "I wish you success in finding an opportunity to continue your education and to attain your academic goals," and, "Though this may be a set-back for you, I do encourage you to continue moving forward. Best of luck in your endeavors." I did move forward. In the direction of pressing the Utah State University dean for admission. I emailed the dean at first, and unsurprisingly, there was no reply. Month after month I would continue to email. Each time expressing my interest to succeed in their program. Finally, *after 11 months,* I suppose the dean grew tired of my emails, and I received a letter in the mail:

Dear Mr. Snow:

I am pleased to inform you that your application has been approved and you have been accepted to the School of Graduate Studies at Utah State University on a provisional matriculation basis.

A what? I was just ecstatic to see the word "approved" but further in the letter it detailed a required B or better or 3.0 grade point average or else: "Failure to meet this requirement will result in termination of your participation in the program."

And would you guess two years later I finished with magna cum laude honors? If you did, you'd guess wrong. Midway through the program, I received a C+ in Accounting Strategies, which dropped my cumulative GPA to 2.95 and prompted another letter letting me know that I was on "probationary matriculated status." With mounting pressure, I somehow pulled A's in Research in Business Decision Sciences and Global Business Strategy, resulting in a final 3.1 GPA. I walked during graduation with the honor of knowing that with persistence even the least book smart kid in his cohort can overcome the odds and achieve a graduate degree.

This is your shot. Take it!

CHAPTER EIGHT

NEVER GIVE UP

"Success is not final, failure is not fatal: it is the courage to continue that counts."

- Winston Churchill

s a mountaineer, I have had experiences that most people cannot (or never want to) envision. I have climbed the highest mountain in the middle of Antarctica in an atmosphere void of dust and pollution, a skyline so clear I saw the bend of the earth across the horizon. I have looked out from the highest points on every continent. I have witnessed both the last moments before death and life-saving acts of heroism. In traveling the world, I have met bold human beings prepared to risk their lives for their ambitions, and developed lifelong friendships with people from cultures I would have never otherwise encountered. I also launched two adventure travel companies, something I couldn't have conceived of just a few years earlier.

All of this would not have happened if I had succumbed to the dismal weather, the fatigue, and the sickness and turned around on that first climb up Mt. Rainier. As I described in Chapter 2, around midnight we set out for the seven-hour continual climb to the summit, painstakingly plowing through the high winds, which are notorious on Mount Rainier: due to its proximity to the ocean and with no protecting mountain ranges nearby, it experiences the full force of any weather system—and our morning was no exception. As we were climbing in the early hours of the morning, we arrived at High Point, a section of exposed glacier where the wind scours the mountainside, picking up ice crystals that slapped us in the face like low-grit sandpaper. It was in this moment that every part of me wanted to turn around, put my back to the wind, and retreat off the mountain. I had never reached any summit of any mountain. I had no idea what that experience was like. I had no concept of why I was doing this. And, honestly, I don't know why I continued. But something within me pressed forward. I didn't know what it was, but I knew that I had to find out why I was on this mountain in the first place—and that why could only be answered on the top.

DON'T LET THE RISKS OVERWHELM YOU

On a cold January day in 2006, I read a flyer at a mountaineering store about an experienced female mountaineer giving a presentation at a local state college 20 miles from my home. That was right at the time I first got into mountaineering, so I made the snowy drive and in a small intimate group listened to mountaineering pioneer Arlene Blum describe how in 1978, she led the first all-woman expedition to the summit of Annapurna.

Annapurna, located in the same Himalayan region as Mt. Everest, is known for its avalanches and is the deadliest mountain in the world with a fatality rate of 32 percent. Blum and her team were prepared for avalanches, but when they were on the mountain, the avalanches were non-stop—like nothing these experienced mountain climbers had ever seen. There were a few very close calls as they were bringing supplies up, and the expedition considered cancelling because of the very real risk that sooner or later somebody was going to die in an avalanche. One member of the expedition did quit, convinced that someone's death from an avalanche was inevitable. The others decided that they would not let the sharply increased risk stop them. As it turned out, they made it safely past the section of avalanches every time. (Unfortunately, two climbers did die on their summit attempt, but it was not from avalanches.)

Persistence is often risky. No matter what the undertaking in which you're engaged, persisting during the hardest times can be costly. By continuing up Mt. Rainier, I was taking a risk—not just from physical danger, but also the risk of eventual defeat, the risk that I was putting myself in harm's way and subjecting myself to misery for no reason. If you start to focus on the risks, retreat in defeat becomes very tempting. Why take risks, maybe for nothing, when it's so easy to go back to camp and have a hot drink in a warm tent?

Of course, that does not mean that risks should be ignored. In fact, it's the opposite. To succeed at something that's risky—and everything worth doing is going to carry some risk—you have to determine how much risk you can tolerate. Risk tolerance is everything in mountaineering. To most people's surprise, I am a very cautious and calculated person. For my wife's 35th birthday, our good friends surprised her by taking her skydiving. I, along with my three girls, were there anxiously watching her suit up when the dive master pointed to me and said, "We've got one more spot, let's get you suited up." I immediately said, "No, thanks, that kind of high-altitude risk-taking is not my thing."

And I was serious. I have no desire to skydive. My wife and daughters love roller coasters, and I'm just fine as a spectator.

To manage our risk tolerance, we must first look for objective vs. subjective hazards—what is the real hazard, and what is the perceived hazard. In other words, for the subjective hazards, we have to ask ourselves, is the level of risk truly what we believe it is? Perhaps we are being too optimistic. Or perhaps we are being too pessimistic. Optimism and pessimism are subjective evaluations of the risk, but they can have real consequences. A pessimistic evaluation of the risk can lead you to give up too easily.

However, if you think on the mountain that optimism is a positive emotion and pessimism is a negative emotion, think again. Optimism can lead you to undervalue the risks and as a result, not take the necessary precautions. As Michael Useem explains in his book, *The Leadership Moment*, "Too much of either can be counterproductive." As a result, the best leaders on the mountain, Useem writes, will mitigate both—they will try to reduce the level of pessimism to encourage persistence, but they will also try to reduce the level of optimism in order to ensure that care is taken. Useem notes that many accidents happen just after the summit has been reached, when the euphoria of the moment makes climbers less careful.

The importance of the mitigation of optimism and pessimism is highlighted in a research study cited by Useem that focused on the 1963 expedition that led to the first four Americans reaching the summit of Everest, including two using a more treacherous West Ridge route rather than the South Col route taken by Hillary and Tenzing. The expedition was long and harrowing, with the four climbers spending more than two months above their base camp. The study revealed that the psychology of the team members relentlessly mitigated their optimism and pessimism: specifically, when the objective risks were lower, the team members became cautious and wary; when the objective risks were high, the team members were more upbeat! As a result, "Their spirits rarely got too high to encourage recklessness or so low as to cause despair," Useem writes.

Most successful people are optimistic risk-takers. But they aren't foolish. They succeed because they are more likely to be cautious when things are going well, while refusing to be beaten down when things are going badly.

This is an essential skill when you hit the wall and your persistence wanes. Now is the time to mitigate your pessimism and be as optimistic as you can.

DO IT FOR SOMEONE ELSE

When we set out to climb Aconcagua, we'd be in the same region of the Andes mountains as the famed Uruguayan Rugby team's plane crash site. If we had time after our climb, our plan was to visit this incredible location. The 1972 crash was famous because the survivors of the crash, mostly members of the rugby team, survived for two-and-a-half months in sub-freezing temperatures without food or water. As described in the best-selling book *Alive!*

(and the subsequent movie), the survivors had no choice but to resort to cannibalism.

Nando Parrado explained why to a New York business audience: "We had to do that. And I can only tell you that 100 percent of you in that situation, not with the minds you have here now, with the minds we had there, would have done exactly the same thing. It's not nice, it's horrible."

Only 19 at the time of the crash, Parrado is now a successful businessman and motivational speaker. It was Parrado and another teammate who eventually saved the survivors by trekking for weeks through the mountains, hoping to find civilization. Every time Parrado and his teammate, who was named Roberto, reached the peak of a mountain, it was only to see more rows of mountains on the other side. Finally, one day when Parrado and Roberto had reached another peak only to see more empty mountains, Roberto was ready to give up. "We are dead, Nando," Roberto told Parrado. "We are dead." But Parrado refused to give up, telling Roberto, "Roberto, I'm going, going forward, I'm not dying here, I'm walking, every step I take will bring me closer to my father." And Parrado continued walking, Roberto followed, and finally one day, the two saw a man with a horse on the other side of a river. They explained who they were, and within hours, helicopters found and rescued the rest of the survivors.

On the plane with Nando Parrado were his mother and sister. They both died in the crash. As far as Parrado's father knew, his wife, daughter, *and son* had died in the crash. Parrado was determined to survive and return to his father.

There are many times in the midst of a major challenge in which you forget that there are other people in the world. All of your focus is aimed at the goal. In the words of international consultant Gerard Westerby, a goal should be kept "against your eyes. Not in your mind. Not in your heart. But 'against your eyes.'"

But sometimes, your intense focus on the goal makes you forget the bigger picture. It's not all about *you, your* goals, *your* success. When you're on the edge of giving up, think about the people who want you to succeed—or who need you to succeed. Would Parrado have had the same desire to live had his father also perished in the crash? Hard to know. But certainly, the desire to see his father again kept him alive through those long icy, hungry days.

HOW COMMITTED ARE YOU TO YOUR SUMMIT?

Sometimes we lie to ourselves. There are times when, for various reasons, we try to convince ourselves that we are doing what we want to do, or that we are truly excited about something, when deep down the commitment does not exist. For example, perhaps we reach for a promotion in the interest of career development—when in fact we are perfectly happy with the job we already have. Perhaps we try to generate enthusiasm for an activity or party that would please our spouse ... when in fact the enthusiasm is just not there.

You might try to fake it until you make it, as the old expression goes, but when you hit a wall, the truth comes out. In other words, if you are not really committed to the goal, you aren't going to be capable of persisting.

A number of years ago, a study was done that examined the persistence of psychology students (psychology researchers often use a research resource close at hand: psychology students!). In this study, 340 new students entering the Indiana University/Purdue University Indianapolis (IUPUI) psychology program over a period of two years filled out questionnaires that measured their certainty in the major (that is, whether they were certain they had chosen the right degree) and their reasons for choosing the major.

The certainty responses went from 1) *totally undecided* to 5) *absolutely certain I'll keep this major to graduation.* The eight reasons in the questionnaire included short-term considerations (they believed they would enjoy the courses, they had received good grades in psychology in the past, they would graduate faster) and long-term considerations (helping others, preparing for graduate school).

The researchers then examined the academic record of the students at least six years after their entrance in the program to determine which ones had persisted (kept the psychology major and graduated with a degree) and which ones had not. Not surprisingly, the research showed that students who were certain they had chosen the right major were persistent in pursuing their degree to completion. Uncertainty undermined persistence.

As for the reasons for choosing the major, neither short-term considerations nor long-term considerations overwhelmingly predicted persistence. The one consistent factor that predicted persistence was preparing for the graduate degree. Students who were committed to getting a graduate degree were more likely to persist in their undergraduate career.

Just like our Bee Gees friend on Denali, if you're not sure you really want the summit or if there is any doubt or any uncertainty about the goal, when conditions rear up and seem insurmountable, you are going to turn around and give up.

I think on that first mountain; my coworker friend, who had suggested climbing Rainier, wasn't really totally committed to the venture. He was a bit like the psychology students who took psychology because they thought they would enjoy the classes. And to tell you the truth, I was not necessarily committed either … until I got on the mountain. And then, deep inside me, *I wanted that summit.*

BALANCING PATIENCE AND IMPATIENCE

Google the phrase "patience and persistence," and you'll get more than 900,000 links to choose from. That's how commonly the phrase appears on the Internet, and how widespread the connection between the two is accepted.

Patience does play a role in persistence—there's no doubt about that. You can argue that persistence requires patience because, by definition, you're persistent when you refuse to give up, even when you don't achieve your goals immediately or in a short timeframe. The connection is clear. If you lose patience, you give up. On many climbs, you often must wait a long time for the weather to clear. My friend and I sat in a tent in Antarctica for six days before weather permitted a summit attempt. The wait is nerve-wracking—will you ever get your chance?—but you can't be impatient. In many other situations, persistence requires patience. Often, new companies rarely make any money their first two or three years in business. You have to be patient, you have to wait for customers to become aware of your existence and give your product or service a try.

At the same time, I don't think patience is always a virtue—and I would certainly not suggest you plan for patience. By that, I mean do everything in your power for the immediate win or you may let an opportunity go by. When I started my Kilimanjaro travel business, I anticipated and planned for customers to come storming to our venture. My partner, Nickson, had traditional slow-and-easy expectations, thinking that we might have some 30-40 clients our first year. Thankfully, I was right. We had 200 clients in our first full year and over 600 clients in year two. Entrepreneurs who are okay with being patient are probably not going to be entrepreneurs for long.

Some of the greatest achievers in history are actually those who don't have patience. Georgia State University professor Mario Feit takes issue with the assumption that democracy is based on patience: that is, that in a democracy, change occurs when you calmly use democratic institutions and processes, letting democracy play out its course. Feit uses the example of Martin Luther King to demonstrate that patience in social change is not always a virtue. According to Feit, one of the central arguments of King's campaign for civil rights was that African-Americans ("negroes" in the terms of that time) had waited *long enough*.

Martin Luther King even wrote a book, *Why We Can't Wait*, which makes this specific time argument. According to Feit, King is arguing that patience—or more specifically what Feit calls "imposed patience"—is used as a tool of oppression. This goes back to the Roman times, when inferior people—slaves, women— were expected to be patient. At the same time, a man's masculinity could be attacked by calling him "patient!" In modern times, King felt, patience was also a tool of power. "The Negro had never really been patient in the pure sense of the word," he writes in *Why We Can't Wait*. "The posture of silent waiting was forced upon him psychologically because he was shackled physically."

It took amazing persistence in the face of entrenched and even violent resistance for Martin Luther King to lead America's civil rights movement. He even paid for that persistence with his life. But that persistence was driven by impatience, not patience.

So, just as the most successful entrepreneurs are impatient, the most successful leaders of social change are equally impatient.

IF IT'S GOING TO BE, IT'S UP TO ME

When you hit the wall, when everything seems to be stacked against you, when you're in the crucible moment of defeat surrounded by what seems to be insurmountable barriers, the difference between defeat and persistence, between turning back or, instead, somehow breaking through the walls, comes down to a single question: whether or not you believe that *you* are in control of what you do—what psychologists call an internal locus of control—or whether you believe instead that what you do and what happens to you depends on forces outside your control—in other words, you have an external locus of control.

When I was climbing Mt. Rainier and I was running on zero energy, coughing up yellow phlegm from bronchitis, battling sandpaper crystals, I had every reason to turn back. But deep inside, I knew that if I didn't make the summit, it would be because I *decided* not to continue. Year after year, Mt. Rainier hovers around a 50 percent summit success rate. I would not have blamed the mountain, or the weather, or my inexperience, or health or anything else. I would have blamed myself. My mindset. My will.

This feeling of being in control, this feeling of knowing that if you don't persist, it's because *you* chose not to persist—not that the choice was out of your hands—is what separates the great achievers from those who never seem to fulfill their promise.

This is proven by academic research into what psychologists call *causal attribution*. Causal attribution refers to the process of attributing the cause of what happens to you or around you. For example, a disturbing number of students fail to complete their degrees—many of them dropping out in the first year of college. Yet, being accepted to college involves an often stringent admission process, which includes academic tests, detailed applications with extensive criteria, and even interviews. Why do so many students make it through this admission process only to be unable to persist and get their degrees? Yes, there are unexpected impediments and challenges that arise, but are they so daunting and insurmountable that students have no choice but to abandon?

In a series of studies, University of Manitoba professor Raymond Perry and his colleagues explored what he called "The Paradox of Failure"—the paradox being that students go through stringent criteria and still fail. In one study, Perry examined one of the key psychosocial differences among students: perceived control—in other words, how much students believe that academic outcomes are within their control or, on the contrary, are subject to factors outside of their control, such as unfair professors, difficult courses, bad luck, and so forth. He found that students who felt in control when they reached college "reported that they tried harder and were more motivated during the year, experienced less boredom and anxiety, used self-monitoring strategies more often, felt more in control of their course assignments, and obtained higher final grades. In a three-year follow-up study, Perry showed that students with high perceived control had better grade point averages (GPAs) and withdrew from fewer courses over a 3-year period."

I think the whole causal attribution is the essence of persistence. Taking complete accountability and control is fundamental with any great win or progress. Looking at the opposite: those who think situations are the reason for their circumstances are the ones who fail.

Of course, as always, there is a threshold to how much you can control. There are perhaps students, for example, who are unqualified to be in the course of study or in the university that they were able to be accepted in. On the mountain, there are times when you have to acknowledge that your summit bid has been taken away from you by stolen oxygen bottles, a malfunctioning oxygen mask, a slower group ahead on the rope, or more commonly, the weather.

However, that threshold of control is higher to an exponential degree than those who refuse to be accountable for their success.

One of the most difficult military training in the world is the training that Army Rangers must go through. The rangers endure extreme hunger, cold, and fatigue. It's common for Rangers in Ranger School to be driven to the point of having hallucinations. And worse. Despite the extreme physical and mental tests they passed to be admitted into Ranger School, Rangers die during the training. As one Ranger who spent seven years in the special forces told an interviewer, "I have been to war twice, once to Iraq and once to Afghanistan, and I rarely have nightmares about that place. My nightmare is of going back to Ranger School where I'm starving and I'm tired and I'm miserable for 68 straight days."

And yet this very same Ranger insists that anyone can make it through Ranger school—or more precisely, this former Special Forces combatant believes that if you want to make it as a Ranger, you can. In the same interview, he says, "Ranger School, in my opinion is, if you don't quit, and you keep working, if you're willing to recycle and go back, it's just one huge suck. You have to work hard. You have to accept the fact that you're going to be miserable every second of every day for 2 1/2 months, but if you can do that, I think anyone can make it through. But I don't think very many people are willing to do the work or have the mindset."

Can everyone make it through Ranger School if they just persist? No. I've never said that everyone can do anything they want as long as they persist. The lesson of this book is *not* that you can reach your life's summits with persistence alone. The core lesson is that to reach life's summits, you must have persistence. And that includes all the foundations of persistence discussed in this book, such as preparation and a good team around you. It includes understanding the psychology of persistence—the psychological barriers that can hold you back, the psychological mindset such as Carol Dweck's mindset that will push forward.

And most of all, it's believing, as the subtitle of this section states, that

If It's Going to Be, It's Up to Me.

EPILOGUE

EVEREST TAKE 2

*That which we persist in doing becomes easier, not that the nature of
the thing has changed, but our ability to do has increased.*

– Ralph Waldo Emerson

Exactly one year to the day from when we failed to summit
Everest in 2017, I stumbled into my tent at Camp 4. Once
again, I was in position for a summit. The familiar open
expanse of Camp 4 spread out before me. Camp 4 is the most visual
representation on the mountain of the savagery with which Mother
Nature attacks climbers. This highest staging point was littered
with shredded tents from previous expeditions, and discarded fuel
canisters and oxygen bottles strewn about. It was a little eerie
scanning the remnants and seeing the tattered traces of the groups
that had traveled before. Gazing out of my tent, my mind was soon
flooded with memories of the disappointment 365 days before at
this exact spot.

However, things were different this year. Last year, we were
the only group attempting the summit on that day, this year we
were among dozens and dozens of climbers and Sherpa guides who
had analyzed the same weather reports. This gave me confidence
that we would be afforded a summit window, allowing us to finish
what we started.

With my friends Fabian and Dan in the tent next door, Tom and I soon settled into our tent, which we shared with Gyaljen, all the while counting the minutes which passed excruciatingly slow— hoping against hope that the unclimbable pressure that squeezes Everest's summit 350 days a year would relax long enough to allow us passage to her summit.

We wait, we wait, we wait, for the dark black of the night.

If you climb too early, then you're spending the entire summit push in the coldest temperatures on the mountain, risking frostbite and sluggish reaction in the interminable cold. So, we had set our mark to depart around 8:30 to 9:00 p.m. Tom and I didn't speak much. Not much was left to be said. I laid down to rest, but my mind could find no respite. Tom sat upright the entire time, fidgeting with gear, thoughts, the pending punishment of another Everest summit attempt. We both had unfinished business, and our anticipation continued to build with every strained breath in and out of our oxygen masks.

Despite looking at my watch every few minutes, and knowing the time was shortly approaching it was still jarring when Temba, our lead guide, hollered from the tent next door that it was time to get ready. It was time. My heart rate accelerated as adrenaline poured through my body. My thoughts, which had been scattered and unfocused, coalesced and shifted into summit mode. I was ready.

I zipped up my summit suit, put on an open-faced balaclava, adjusted my oxygen mask, put on a thin liner glove, insulated gloves, and then a shell glove, stored a backpack with two liters of water (1/2 liter bottle which I tucked in my summit suit front pocket), strapped on my crampons, buckled the harness around my waist, and took a step into the dark white. Unlike our group blazing solo the previous year, as mentioned, this year we were in a crowd of dozens of climbers and their summit Sherpas, all leaving Camp 4 within 30 minutes of each other; the queue to tie into the first rope section quickly stacked up. We climbed for an hour before reaching a point where the crowd started to thin. Slower climbers needed to step aside and try to regain their breath. Others adjusted their gloves, harness, or ascenders. I witnessed at least two climbers turn back and begin their descent, knowing they didn't have it in them.

One of our Sherpa guides, Dandu, who somehow managed to be the lead climber on our rope, was not fit to be heading for the summit, and continued to go slower and slower. After two hours of climbing slower than our group was capable, and feeling the cold attacking our extremities with this glacial pace, I finally had the difficult task of telling Temba (who is his brother), that Dandu needed to retreat. It was evident to all, but not without consequence. This was the second year in a row that Dandu had made it to summit day, but failed on the actual climb to reach the top. The health and success of the team was at stake. High mountains are unforgiving, and with a painful decision, Temba made the call to turn Dandu around. With either relief or disappointment, Dandu descended back to Camp 4.

For the entire expedition Dan (who is 10 years older than Tom, Fabian or I) climbed faster than us at every stage, and summit day was no exception. He and one of our Sherpas, Dawa, were able to move ahead of Dandu just before Dandu slowed us to a crawl.

Climbing into the dark, at a renewed pace, we stopped just below the Balcony to exchange for fresh oxygen bottles and were reunited with Dan and Dawa. It was a shock, since our slowed pace had put them far ahead of us. When Dan removed his goggles, the goggle inadvertently caught his right eye and knocked out one of his contact lenses. He tried in vain to find it. Also, when he bit into an energy bar, it stuck into a tooth and popped off a permanent cap, exposing a live ground-down stump. That was enough to slow the charging bull of a climber that is Dan.

I was pleased that the four of us could now climb together. Especially since we were approaching the Tenzing Step, a rock formation I was all too familiar with. This was the section last season where rocks were breaking around us and we tied into the wrong ropes, which proved perilous. This year, there was some commotion above that stalled our progress. A Chinese climber picked the wrong time and place to contemplate where he was and what he was doing, and in so doing, stalled the entire mountain behind him. Fabian minced no words in letting him know he needed to get climbing or get off the rope. That was enough to get the log jam moving again.

Continuing our climb, we shortly arrived at the South Summit. A year and one day after I had stood at the exact same spot. The previous year, we'd arrived at 3:30 in the morning, while it was still pitch black. This year, we were there around 5:00 a.m., with the first morning light illuminating the southeast ridge and revealing the remaining 300 vertical feet that eluded us the year before. I was in front of our group by this time, and I leaned down to start warming my phone and camera batteries when I noticed that my GPS tracker had frozen solid, rendering it useless. How long had it been off? Did my world as I knew it back home, which was hanging on every screen update, know it had frozen? I opened some hand warmers, stuck them on the back near its battery, and within minutes, it powered on. I would later learn our cheerleaders back home shouted for joy when the frozen tracker that had disappeared for four hours shot back to life and displayed to those back home that we were only a few "inches" from the summit.

I was very upset the tracker had stopped signaling, as I knew the free world that was following my track would be worried why I wasn't progressing up the mountain. The same group of family and friends had, just a year before, watched in disbelief as our tracker began reversing short of the summit, depression setting in as they knew what it meant for our attempt. Later, I learned that the signal stopped sending just a few hours out of Camp 4. Many texts were sent back and forth between those closest to me about what it meant. Fortunately, my wife was tracking Dan's GPS receiver as well, and my brother-in-law texted the family that "there was no way that 'D' would stop while Dan climbed on. He is too strong and prepared." It was with great relief when the signal went through and showed me just short of the summit.

About this time, the wind began to unleash, and the trauma along with the gale of last year swept into my summit suit. Tom was also feeling the nerves, and on a particularly exposed section, looked back at Dan and said, "I don't know about this. Looks kind of marginal." Dan snapped back confidently, "Let's just get it done!"

The final summit ridge is unnerving, to say the least. Make a mistake to your right and there's a 10,000-foot drop into China. Fumble tying into the rope to your left and there's an 8,000-foot fall back to Nepal. This is one of the few places on earth where you have time to contemplate your death before you arrive! Make every step count. Make every step count. Execute every transition perfectly. Experience and talent rise to the forefront, and those who have it do just that.

(Later, when I got home from Everest, my brother-in-law Rob asked me, "At what point did you know you would reach the summit?" Without hesitation and with a wry smile I said, "The moment we touched down in Kathmandu.")

This year, we would not be denied. We pushed forward, cursing the wind one moment and asking for forgiveness the next; to our amazement and I'm sure the answered prayers from our team back home, the winds abated.

By the time we neared the top, it was perfectly still. We arrived. The four of us, linked arm in arm, took synchronized steps until there we were standing on the most famous piece of real estate on earth.

Along with our three Sherpa guides, Temba, Gyaljen, and Dawa, we staked claim to a spot two feet below the summit, and all of us plopped down, embracing in a gigantic hug.

It was a sweet moment for me and Gyaljen; a year before, as I was slumped over, defeated and weeping at Camp 2, Gyaljen comforted me and pointed up to Everest which we could see from our dining tent door and said, "It will still be there, David dai. If you come back, I will guide with you again."

Fabian had his satellite phone, and we each made a call to our loved ones.

I made a video on my cell phone thanking friends and family, Sange, and Brooklyn, Ellie, Sadie and the love of my life, Tiffany. They were with me every step of the way.

We had arrived in Kathmandu airport April 19, and we were on the summit May 18. While it still took a month, we were the fastest group of the season on this route. And while we climbed for a month, we were on the summit less than 30 minutes. As we gathered our gear to prepare for the descent, Tom, Dan and Fabian started down, and I stood and took a moment, holding my breath, looking around and giving a silent prayer of gratitude for this experience. For what this summit and all the Seven Summits had taught me. For what it had provided me. Like so many others who have stepped down from this spot, life would be changed forever.

Back in Colorado, Sange was following our every step and was the first to post on social media (after my wife) that his "buddy had successful summiting top of the world Mt. Everest. Safe descent and see you soon in US." Sange Sherpa continues to heal and inspire. He is a bright light wherever he goes. Sange's determination to continue his charge forward on the mountain has led to his desire to return home. To be amongst the beauty of the

Himalayas and his siblings. He has a desire to start his own Himalayan adventure company. He also wants to return to the big peaks again, and, knowing his determination, he'll be on top of the world in any pursuit.

You get one shot at this thing called life. Explore the unknown places. It's there you'll discover the most meaningful relationships. Every mountain top I've stood upon I've had close friends by my side. In the end, that is what this climb is all about. And if you ever get a chance to stand on life's summits, whatever that is for you, take that step. Because you never know where it might lead.

REFERENCES

CHAPTER ONE: NO SUMMIT WITHOUT PERSISTENCE

James Dyson

Dinah Eng. "How James Dyson Created a $3 Billion Vacuum Empire." *Fortune.* September 9, 2017.

Fred Whelan and Gladys Stone. "James Dyson: How Persistence Leads to Success." *Huffington Post.* Updated December 6, 2017.

Sylvester Stallone

Aly Weisman. "Dirt-Poor Sylvester Stallone Turned Down $300,000 In 1976 To Ensure He Could Play 'Rocky.'" *Business Insider.* April 2, 2014.

Tom Ward. "The Amazing Story Of The Making Of 'Rocky.'" *Forbes.* October 14, 2017.

Sylvester Stallone interview on The Graham Norton Show. January 17, 2014.

J.K. Rowling

J.K. Rowling. "The Fringe Benefits of Failure and the Importance of Imagination." Harvard commencement address. *Harvard Magazine.* June 5, 2008.

Erik Weihenmayer

In addition to personal knowledge and experience:

Christine Wang. "Erik Weihenmayer: The only way to climb Everest is to go do it." *CNBC.* April 4, 2004.

Gina Dimuro. "Erik Weihenmayer: The Man Who Summited Everest — While Blind." *All That's Interesting blog.* August 2, 2018.

https://erikweihenmayer.com/

https://erikweihenmayer.com/about-erik/

CHAPTER TWO: THE PERSISTENCE MINDSET

Carol Dweck research

Clifton B Parker. "Perseverance key to children's intellectual growth, Stanford scholar says." *Stanford News.* April 29, 2015. Carol Dweck. *Mindset: The New Psychology of Success.* New York: Random House, 2006.

Stress Mindset Measure study

Alia J. Crum, Peter Salovey and Shawn Anchor. "Rethinking Stress: The Role of Mindsets in Determining the Stress Response." *Journal of Personality and Social Psychology.* 2013.

Karl Turk

Gregg Doyel. "Arlington grad Turk overcomes paralysis to coach." *Indianapolis Star.* January 6, 2015.

Lee Ridley

Amy Brookbanks and Carl Greenwood. "Britain's Got Talent winner Lost Voice Guy reveals 'I didn't have any friends as a child and my iPad saved me.'" *The Sun.* June 6, 2018.

The Disability Mindset

Dan Jolivet. "The disability mindset: what it is and how to overcome it." *Workplace Possibilities blog.* April 12, 2018.

Joy Mangano

Marguerite Ward. "Inventor Joy Mangano has sold $3 billion of products and says this is the biggest myth about success." *CNBC.* November 25, 2017.

CHAPTER THREE: CHOOSE YOUR ROPE TEAM

Airplane Insulin story

"IIT-Kanpur student says engineering skills helped save man's life on flight." *Hindustan Times.* May 11, 2018.

Dave Winsborough research

Dave Winsborough and Tomas Chamorro-Premuzic. "Great Teams Are About Personalities, Not Just Skills." *Harvard Business Review.* January 2017.

Dave Winsborough. *Fusion: The Psychology of Teams.* Tulsa, OK: Hogan Assessments, 2017.

Matthew James research

Matthew B. James, Ph.D. "Stop Letting Negative People Drag You Down." *Huffington Post.* May 13, 2014.

Bill George

Peter Sims. "True North Groups: A Conversation with Bill George." *Harvard Business Review.* September 13, 2011.

Bill George and Doug Baker. *True North Groups: A Powerful Path to Personal and Leadership Development.* San Francisco: Berrett-Koehler Publishers, 2011.

Chapter Four: Preparing Your Pack

Locke and Latham research

"Locke's Goal-Setting Theory." *Mind Tools blog.*

Edwin A. Locke, Gary P. Latham, Ken J. Smith and Robert E. Wood. *A Theory of Goal Setting and Task Performance.* New York: Pearson College Div., 1990.

Peter Guber

Peter Guber. "Career Curveballs: The Uncertain Pitch Can Be Your Home Run." *PeterGuber.com.*

Peter Guber biography. *IMDB.com.*

Warren Buffett

Alice Schroeder. *The Snowball: Warren Buffett and the Business of Life.* New York: Bantam, 2009 (Update Edition).

Plan B study

Jihae Shin and Katherine Milkman. "How Backup Plans Can Harm Goal Pursuit: The Unexpected Downside of Being Prepared for Failure." *Organizational Behavior and Human Decision Processes.* July 2016.

Planning Fallacy research

Roger Buehler, Dale Griffin, and Michael Ross. "Exploring the "Planning Fallacy.: Why People Underestimate Their Task Completion Times. *Journal of Personality and Social Psychology.* 1994.

CHAPTER FIVE: IT STARTS FROM THE OUTSIDE IN

Ruben Meerman

"How breathing and metabolism are interconnected." Ruben Meerman. TEDxBundaberg.

Jesus Peteiro

quoted in: Sarah Klein. "This Simple Stair Test Could Predict Your Risk of Dying." *Health.com.* December 06, 2018.

Amy Cuddy

Amy Cuddy. *Presence: Bringing Your Boldest Self to Your Biggest Challenges.* New York: Little, Brown, 2015.

CHAPTER SIX: THE DARK SIDE OF PERSISTENCE

Shriya Shah-Klorfine

"Mt. Everest: Into the Death Zone." The Fifth Estate. 2012.

Hiroo Onoda

"Hiroo Onoda – obituary." *The Telegraph.* April 14, 2017.

Suzanne Raga

Suzanne Raga. "8 Tips for Dealing with Pushy Salespeople." *Mental Floss.com.* December 6, 2016.

Peter Caputa

Peter Caputa. "When Does Sales Persistence Turn Into Harassment?" *Hubspot.com.* Updated July 28, 2017.

Niti Shah

Niti Shah. "How to be Persistent in Sales Without Annoying Your Prospects." *Hubspot.com.* October 26, 2018.

Dan Rockwell

Dan Rockwell. "7 Ways to Stop Being Hardheaded. *Leadership Freak blog.* November 10, 2015.

Blackberry

Sean Silcoff, Jacquie McNish and Steve Ladurantaye. "How BlackBerry blew it: The inside story." *The Globe and Mail.* Originally published September 27, 2013, updated online April 7, 2018.

CHAPTER SEVEN: DON'T ALMOST

Olympic Medalists research

David Matsumoto and Bob Willingham. "The thrill of victory and the agony of defeat: Spontaneous expressions of medal winners of the 2004 Athens Olympic Games." *Journal of Personality and Social Psychology.* October 2006.

Jason G. Goldman. "Why Bronze Medalists Are Happier Than Silver Winners." *Scientific American.* August 9, 2012.

Tom Bourdillon

Mick Conefrey. *Everest 1953: The Epic Story of the First Ascent.* Seattle, WA: Mountaineers Books, 2014.

Andy McSmith. "The History Man: The tale of Tom Bourdillon." *The Independent.* September 15, 2008.

Counterfactual Thinking

"The Benefit of Counterfactual Thinking." *Psychology Today.* Originally published July 1, 1995, updated June 9, 2016.

Keith Markman, Matthew McMullen, and Ronald Elizaga. "Counterfactual thinking, persistence, and performance: A test of the Reflection and Evaluation Model." *Journal of Experimental Social Psychology.* 2008.

Dan Marino

Adam H. Beasley. "Marino's One Regret." *Miami Herald.* August 18, 2015.

Allianz "Gift of Life" research

"One-Third of Americans Regret Major Life Choices, But Many Embrace Newfound Opportunity to 'Rechart' Course." *Allianz press release.* May 23, 2016.

Davidai and Gilovich research

Shai Davidai and Tom Gilovich. "The ideal road not taken: The self-discrepancies involved in people's most enduring *regrets.*" *Emotion.* 2018.

Lila MacLellan. "A new study on the psychology of persistent regrets can teach you how to live now." *qz.com.* June 10, 2018.

Susan Kelley. "Woulda, Coulda, Shoulda: The Haunting Regret of Failing Our Ideal Selves." *Cornell Chronicle*. May 23, 2018.

CHAPTER EIGHT: NEVER GIVE UP

Optimism and Pessimism

Michael Useem. *The Leadership Moment*. New York: Crown Business, 1998.

Nando Parrado

"Crisis Management and Living Life." Speech at World Business Forum. New York City. 2010.

Gerard Westerby

Gerard Westerby. *In Hostile Territory: Business Secrets of a Mossad Combatant*. New York: HarperBusiness, 1998.

Persistence of Psychology Students study

Barbara S. Metzner, Joan B. Lauer, and D.W. Rajecki. "Predicting Persistence among Psychology Majors at an Urban University." *North American Journal of Psychology*. 2003.

Patience In Democracy research

Mario Feit. "Democratic impatience: Martin Luther King, Jr. on democratic temporality." *Contemporary Political Theory*. 2016.

The Paradox of Failure research

Tara L. Haynes, Raymond P. Perry, Robert H. Stupnisky, and Lia M. Daniels. "A Review of Attributional Retraining Treatments: Fostering Engagement and Persistence in Vulnerable College Students." chapter in J.C. Smart (ed.), *Higher Education:*

Handbook of Theory and Research. New York: Springer Science + Business Media, 2009.

Persistence through Ranger School

Eric Barker. "5 Lessons from a Special Ops Soldier on Leadership and Persistence." *Barking Up the Wrong Tree blog.* Feb 13, 2013.

ACKNOWLEDGMENTS

There's a risk with acknowledgements, knowing that I'll miss someone important, but then again, this is a book about risks!

Most importantly, I am grateful to God for His wisdom and direction. For prayers answered and delayed, for His correct timing. For the trust to serve and to receive service from His children across every incredible continent He created.

I am grateful for my mother, Connie. Her quiet example of never giving up, making the best of the worst, and always supporting me in anything I set out to do keeps me reaching higher even today.

I am grateful for my climbing friends who took the step, climbed by my side, and weathered the storms across the Seven Summits: Tom Wilkinson, Brandon Fisher, Larry Daugherty, Cecil Groetken, Dan Stringham, Fabian Fabbro, Jared Butler, Jason Shurtleff, Luke Humphrey, Rich Bliss, Alex Stayer, Talmage Price, Tosh Rymer, Andrew Butterworth, Jenny Schumacher and even Jarret.

I am grateful for the guides who led the way and helped me discover so much more than just the summit: Goodluck Charles, Juani Tomaselli, Alexander Eliseev, Lhakpa Sherpa, Gyaljen Sherpa, Temba Sherpa, Dawa Sherpa, Sange Sherpa and the late Sarki Sherpa. Your leadership and selfless service have altered my very DNA of what's possible.

I am forever indebted to The Dudes; childhood friends who shaped who I became.

I am grateful for my older siblings who made this youngest kid fight for every laugh.

I am grateful for my father, who never called in sick and who taught me the value of discipline.

I am grateful for my endless in-laws with their all-encompassing support.

I am grateful for the direction and insights of Chris Murray and Rob Richards. Your brainstorming and wordsmith abilities far surpassed anything I could have done on my own.

I am so grateful and beyond blessed for my house full of girls. My daughters Brooklyn, Ellie, and Sadie are a support, an inspiration and motivation for all that I strive to become.

And to my wife, Tiffany, thank you for taking this journey into the unknown with me. I wasn't a climber when we met. I was a broke college student with two jobs and selling plasma so we could eat macaroni. Your support and faith have meant the world to me.

Thank you for being with me every step of the way.

ABOUT THE AUTHOR

The rare combination of international adventurer and entrepreneur, David Snow is one of a handful of people in the world who has organized and led teams to the Seven Summits—including two expeditions of Mt. Everest—and directed his passion for mountaineering to build a multimillion-dollar adventure travel company, leading the way for thousands of adventurers to realize their dreams.

He draws from his unique experiences and achievements to deliver memorable and relevant takeaways to corporate and civic groups about defining and attaining success, effective leadership in dynamic environments, and aligning goals to persist through any obstacle.

David lives in the foothills of the Wasatch Mountains outside of Salt Lake City, Utah with his wife and three daughters.

To find out more about David's presentations or next adventures, visit:

www.davidgsnow.com

Made in the USA
Middletown, DE
04 September 2024